READING MY MIND

Testimonials for Reading My Mind

Reading My Mind is an amazing and incredibly accurate account of our journey at a Prestigious College twenty years ago. Mary has provided a great roadmap for students on how to navigate college life, in addition to highlighting certain routes on the map not to take, haha. It's a great read for students and parents alike and a must-have to include in your student's second semester care package. It's everything you want; it's everything you need...

—Ryan (Yes, that Ryan)

Previously, before reading this book, I feared traveling over 1,500 miles to attend an out-of-state University. After reading this book, I am now excited to experience new things and make new memories. This book made me realize that my life has just begun and that I'm ready for any obstacles that come my way.

—Madi H., Age 18

This book brings back some great memories. Mary offers great advice to those exploring new adventures.

—Jimmy Adams

I wish I had this book available when I went to college! It would have helped so much!

—Daniela Barreto

Whether in music, law or writing, Mary has always succeeded as a performer and shares inspirational messages beneficial to others.

—Joel Hoekstra of Whitesnake, Trans Siberian Orchestra

Reading Mary's unedited journal entries brought me down our winding and hilly memory lane of college and coming of age. Mary lays bare her inner thoughts and soul in this book, in which we explore, and for some of us re-examine, choices made, relationships engaged in, and experiences that have forever left their mark and made us who we are today. For some, this book provides an opportunity to look back and fondly reflect on the transformative times of young adulthood. For others, this book serves as a guide for what they do not tell you about life after high school. Mary invites us on her journey of self-discovery and we are lucky enough to join the ride and even do some self-discovery of our own along the way.

—Carolyn Razon-Fernandez, Ph.D.

I am so happy I read this book before heading off to college.

—Elise C., Age 19

READING MY MIND

*WHILE YOU ARE READING MY MIND, I WANT YOU TO BE
EVERYTHING YOU HAVE DREAMT YOU WOULD BE.*

MARY REID

PYP **Publish**
Your Purpose

For permission requests, write to the publisher, addressed "Attention: Permissions Coordinator," at the address below.

Publish Your Purpose
141 Weston Street, #155
Hartford, CT, 06141

PYP **Publish**
Your Purpose

The opinions expressed by the Author are not necessarily those held by Publish Your Purpose.

Ordering Information: Quantity sales and special discounts are available on quantity purchases by corporations, associations, and others. For details, contact the publisher at hello@publishyourpurpose.com.

Edited by: Elliott Tapia-Kwan, August Li, Emily Ribeiro
Cover design by: Rebecca Pollock
Typeset by: Jet Launch

ISBN: 979-8-88797-078-3 (hardcover)
ISBN: 979-8-88797-079-0 (paperback)
ISBN: 979-8-88797-080-6 (ebook)

Library of Congress Control Number: 2023915086

First edition, November, 2023

The information contained within this book is strictly for informational purposes. The material may include information, products, or services by third parties. As such, the Author and Publisher do not assume responsibility or liability for any third-party material or opinions. The publisher is not responsible for websites (or their content) that are not owned by the publisher. Readers are advised to do their own due diligence when it comes to making decisions.

Publish Your Purpose is a hybrid publisher of non-fiction books. Our mission is to elevate the voices often excluded from traditional publishing. We intentionally seek out authors and storytellers with diverse backgrounds, life experiences, and unique perspectives to publish books that will make an impact in the world. Do you have a book idea you would like us to consider publishing? Please visit PublishYourPurpose.com for more information.

Dedicated to:

Dennis & Carol

My experiences would be nothing without you.

CONTENTS

FOREWORD

In 2005, when I was still young and full of bravado, I wrote a book with my brother based on the idea that at some point in our lives, we stop creating new memories and start relying on old ones. Fast forward almost 20 years, and I'm about to hit the big 5-0, the age where you're supposed to be telling the same old stories over and over again, just so you don't forget what it was like when you were young. The age where all the fun is reserved for the kids, and responsibility weighs you down like a ton of bricks. The age where life is over. Or so I thought.

Turns out, I couldn't have been more wrong. Life is not just about living in the past. Every one of us has a past full of memories, a life we are living right now, and a future full of possibilities. Sure, we can't change the past, but hopefully, we'll look back on it with pride, laughter, and lessons learned. The present is where it's at. It will never be right now again, so we have to make sure we savor every moment. And then there's the future. I was so wrong about the future—it's not all downhill from here. There's so much to look forward to in life, and it's not a zero-sum game. The plan for a happy future is simple: being present in the moment and making the most of today will create the memories you're proud of for tomorrow.

Life is full of stages, each with its own unique opportunities, realities, and responsibilities. In our early years, we learn, we make great friends, and we deal with some not-so-great ones. We come to realize that family is everything, every day, forever. We figure out who we are, who we should be, what makes us happy, and who we should listen to (hint: our parents are usually a good place to start). As we progress through life, we hit a stage where it's time to really try new things.

Most of the decisions we make at this point affect the short term. The most important things in life seem to be "what should I do tonight?" and "how can I get into that party?" But this stage is all about balance—pushing the limits without limiting our opportunities in the future. And then responsibility hits. We're on our own, our parents are no longer our fallback, and it's time to take hold of our true fate. We're forced to think beyond today and tomorrow and consider the longer term. Where do we want to live? What kind of career do we want? What sort of relationship do we want to be in? Through it all, we must never forget the magic formula: memories and experiences of the past, plus making the most of today, equals a good future.

As for me, I'm in my late forties now. My responsibilities have changed, and I'm certainly not doing what I did in my twenties and thirties. But I still have so much to look forward to—traveling with my wife, experiences with my kids, getting together with family and lifelong friends, making new memories, and laughing until it hurts.

Now, let me introduce you to my cousin, Mary (Burke) Reid. I have a lot of cousins, so I'll never pick a favorite, but Mary is definitely up there. We've had a lot of fun together—from decades of Christmas Eve gatherings to celebrating St. Patrick's Day every year at our family's Irish pub to what seems like a gajillion weddings, to an infamous trip to New York City (which you'll read about). Mary has always amazed me with her tenacity and her ability to create experiences. She's not just a one-time winner of radio show concert ticket giveaways—she's the crowned champion of free tickets. She'll try out for Family Feud without a second thought, and she's not afraid to make out with her cousin's handsome friend. "(Okay, maybe we shouldn't talk about that one.)"

But the moment that blew my mind was this: We were having a not-so-unusual boozy lunch with our dads and respective uncles at the famous Italian Village Bar. After a couple of hours, Mary asked me if we could go have a few more drinks. (As if we hadn't had enough already!) Arm twisted (not difficult), I agreed. And that's when Mary dropped a bombshell. She had been writing in her journal every day, for her entire life. I was amazed. She was thinking about writing a book based on her journal. I was never more excited for her. She had to do it! Why not? At that moment, I realized how aligned Mary and I are. Mary's journal is the formula. She not only was memorializing her life, she was forcing herself to live in the moment. If she were to write every day, she might as well create good stories to write about! And Mary's journal serves as the fuel to give her something to look forward to in the future.

Mary's journey through life, as detailed in her book, is a gift to the reader. As you read through the pages, discover opportunities to take action in your own life. This is not a book that you should read and think "yeah, one day I'll do something like that." Start now. With that in mind, here are some prompts to get you started:

- What are three or four things that make you laugh? What stories do you tell your family and friends? Follow Mary's path to gather meaning and joy from the many moments in life.
- What could you do more of in life? How about things you should do less? Use the guidance and lessons learned from Mary's experiences to reflect on your own.
- How can you make the most of tomorrow? Imagine if you had to write about your day, every day before you went to bed. How would you ensure you had something exciting to write about? While we all might not be as diligent as Mary's daily journaling, we can all be inspired by how she filled her days with worthwhile journal entries.

Reading My Mind is not just a book, it's a survival guide for life. And Mary's message is not about living in the past or worrying about the future. The hope is that every reader's day, one by one, becomes better than the last. And remember, you'll always regret what you didn't do more than what you did do. Unless of course, we're talking about that tattoo from spring break or letting your friends pick your karaoke song.

—Michael Burke, co-author, along with Tim Burke, of *Die Happy: 499 Things Every Guy's Gotta Do While He Still Can*

INTRODUCTION

The summer before I headed off to college, many people told me college would be the best four years of my life (they were right). The only way I felt that I could capture these years was by journaling. The excerpts from my journals are original masterpieces, written nightly before I retired to bed (or passed out). The entries have not been edited. There are some entries I wish I'd edited, but that would defeat the purpose of this book. This book does not consist of rules or regulations, just experiences and advice to those heading off to college or encountering new adventures. Of course, as they say, hindsight is twenty-twenty but I am hopeful my advice can be beneficial to you.

The events of this book take place at a Prestigious College on the East Coast, so let's go with PC for short. It provided a home for four very short years, lifelong friends, beautiful coastlines, and a funny accent.

Before diving in, here is a quick summary of my childhood. I was raised in an Irish Catholic family, the youngest of three children. My brother, Dennis, is five years older than me and my sister, Kathy, is two years older than me. We were all raised with a strict, no-nonsense upbringing. Luckily, my siblings paved the way, walked the line so I could witness what I could and could not get away with. I watched both siblings take a semester off from college for different reasons, to my father's dismay. I had decided at that moment I had to go far away and graduate in four years.

The three of us kids witnessed our parents working their tails off to provide a house and higher education. We would all strive for their approval. Graduating college without a break would certainly achieve said approval.

My mom was a nurse and my father, a lawyer. My mom admirably received two master's degrees while raising three young children. My father practiced law for twenty-five years with his two brothers before becoming a judge. They were always reaching for more. My parents instilled a remarkable work ethic within my siblings and I; from a young age I was taught if you wanted something, you must work for it. Nothing was given to us (besides the essentials); it was earned. I am grateful for that early lesson as it has stuck with me.

In high school, I sadly only attended a handful of parties, and even with those, had to lie to my parents to get out of the house. I believe the problem was that I attended a private high school forty minutes from home, and my high school friends lived across the greater Chicagoland area. A lot of driving would have been involved and I guess they (correctly) presumed I would probably drink and drive my way to and from said parties. (They are pretty smart people). Remember that Uber, Lyft, and every other ride-sharing service was nonexistent at this time. Not to mention, I was admittedly sheltered. Don't worry, I absolutely made up for it in college.

One family I regularly babysat for bought their son and me pool passes. The local swimming pool had six diving boards, consisting of a half-meter board all the way up to the high dive, which stood ten feet above the water. I never really paid attention to those boards until that summer and gasped when I saw a girl doing a very pretty "jackknife." If you are not up to speed with the latest diving terminology, a jackknife is when you walk to the end of the board, hurdle up one leg to gain some height, and then, while in midair, bend down, touch your toes, and enter the water headfirst. I vividly remember saying to myself *I want to do that!* And so, as with any other challenge presented to me, I vowed to learn how to do a jackknife and a plethora of other dives.

After that summer at the pool and as I entered my sophomore year of high school, I gladly gave up softball and asked the swim coach if I could join the diving team. The problem was that our high school did not have a diving team, but, because divers competed and earned points for the swim team, it was in the coach's best interest to *have* a diving team. The other minor problem was that our school did not have a diving board, either. But not to worry—my school sent me to the rival school to train with *their* diving coach in *their* pool. I simply did not care about *where* I was diving–I just wanted to learn how to dive. My dad admired my dedication and found a superstar diving coach. Every Sunday, he would drive me out to Munster, Indiana and I would practice with Chuck Chelich's diving team. I was so determined to learn and compete. Soon after, I found a club team up north where I trained my junior and senior years of high school. Thankfully, the high school hired a wonderful diving coach my senior year. I finally had a solid diving list, and Coach Eric took me to Sectionals, where I placed third.

During my senior year of high school, various college representatives gave presentations about why one should attend their school. If you wanted to attend their pitch, you had a free pass from class. When my friend asked if we should ditch English class and attend PC's pitch, it was a no-brainer.

I had never heard of PC in my life, let alone ever traveled to the East Coast, but the college representative quickly caught my attention when he said it was a small school on the East Coast and had a Division I swimming and diving team. I literally knew, at that moment, this was the school for me. I begged my parents to take me for a visit. As soon as we stepped on campus, my gut feeling was confirmed. My mom, however, felt the campus was a little too far from home.

I believe what sealed the deal was that PC offered a small music scholarship if I continued studying piano and participated in their music program. I had been playing the piano since I was eight years old and was happy to continue studying music. This was the only school to have offered money, and my parents thankfully took the bait. I received a large white envelope in December, 1998 and screamed when I read the first line welcoming me to the PC Class of 2003! I think I started packing right away and could not wait to start my college adventure.

FRESHMAN YEAR

1

FREEDOM RINGS

I stared at the sun to avoid crying while hugging my mom goodbye. I had successfully hugged my dad without shedding a tear, but my mom and I had become really close in the last few months, and I was trying hard to keep it together. If I started to cry, she would start to cry, and then they would never leave. My dad, mom, and I had just spent a grueling seventeen hours driving from Chicago to PC. I sat against the car door, somewhat squooshed against the window to allow room for my most beloved items. I was one hug away from being "free"–endless parties and no one to come home to at night. No driving. No curfew. No questions. Pure freedom. Certainly, I was scared and anxious. I was being dropped a thousand miles away and being left to discover this strange new world on my own, but I was up for the challenge.

I watched my parents drive away and did my best to act natural. I had to pretend I was not in awe of this vast campus. I suddenly had to navigate my way around on my own. I was assigned to live near the tallest building on campus–so I used that building as my point of reference. I have zero sense of direction and found myself lost a handful of times the first week. I was just taking the scenic route. Find your grounding and go from there.

Being on the swimming and diving team automatically gave me thirty swimming and diving friends. I was very lucky to land in a place and immediately become part of a family. I would highly suggest joining a team or club. There was an instant bond with my teammates, which I still have to this day.

A week before I arrived on campus, I received an invitation in the mail (yes, that was how it was done back then) for the annual "All Around the World Party" hosted by the swimming and diving team. I had not even arrived on campus and was already invited to a party! I was ecstatic. I could not wait! About a week after my parents dropped me off and just as I caught my breath, it was time to party.

September 10, 1999

So then tonight was the ALL AROUND THE WORLD party. We first went to Maggie's and the[y] poured vodka, apple juice, cinnamon, then whip cream into our mouths. Then I went to Mandy's, where we had to do straight vodka shots with lemons & sugar. Then we went to Greg's and he is coming to Chicago with me!! Then we went to Matt's & I don't remember the rest! Talk to you later.

That first college party was nothing short of amazing—we were walking down the street holding our drinks. We were drinking. In public. It was so strange and terrifying because I did not want to get caught—but drinking while walking down the street on a Friday night in a college town quickly became the norm, and I embraced it!

It is sometimes challenging, but imperative, to practice moderation while in college. While I personally knew some who partied literally every night during freshman year, most or all of them did not return second semester. And as everyone had told me that college is the best four years, *you need to practice moderation.* Do not drink all the alcohol at once. Do not skip all your classes. Do not skip all your practices. Finding a good balance takes hard work and determination, but four years is much better than one semester.

Each week I was more comfortable at PC. My classes were not as challenging as imagined, except for Western Civilization. "Civ" was a two-year class. If you did not pass it freshman year, you had to repeat it, which instilled enough fear to make you pass. I was also taking sociology and English classes as I needed to declare my major by soph-omore year and was sure I would be a lawyer one day. I had agreed to continue studying music and was taking piano lessons with an extraor-dinary teacher from Romania. What started as my parents thinking piano would be a great instrument for a kid to learn grew into my passion and opportunity to escape within the music. The music hall on campus always seemed open. I would lock myself in a room and play the piano for hours. You could have found me in any of those rooms whenever I needed a break or just an escape from reality.

Music has always played a huge part in my life. I competed in state competitions while in high school. I also regularly babysat for a well-known musician, who frequently had other well-known musi-cians in his home studio, while I watched his son. He played every summer at nearby festivals. I was given money to keep his son enter-tained with the rides and games and was also given a backstage pass so that we could freely come and go. I watched many shows backstage with his (gorgeous) wife and was simply in awe of the music and per-formances in front of the roaring crowds. I wanted music to be my life, I just did not know *how.* My dad reminded me working in the music industry was "one in a million" and steered me towards studying law. I witnessed his success. Because it was tangible, I grasped onto the thought of being an attorney one day, even though deep down inside, I wanted to make a career out of music.

I am still perplexed as to why college students need to declare their major and studies so early. I was still finding my way and, while I thought I was going to be an attorney, was still navigating courses to determine what I really wanted to do. Do not feel pressured to know exactly what you want to do for the rest of your life. It changes. Let yourself breathe and grow before you declare your future. You have time. And if you have declared your major with confidence, then I applaud you. You are ahead of the game!

I started successfully navigating my way around campus. I had strong friendships with my fellow diving teammates, along with the girls across the hall–but unfortunately not with my roommates.

Athletes were assigned to a specific dorm. We did not have fraternities or sororities at PC, however, if you were an athlete, you were assigned to live in the on-campus athlete dorms. But I thought I was wiser than the brilliant college administrators, chose to override their suggestion, and found myself in a non-athlete dorm, in a very small room, with *three* other girls, Meg, Jenn, and Liz. That is a lot of girls for a small space. I stupidly agreed to live with a girl I had gone to high school with. Do not do that. It seemed safe at the time. Not to mention, we were in separate social circles. My thought process was *Hooray, I already know someone from high school and we are going to live together.* Don't. Do. That. Leave it at the *I already know someone from high school.* That is good enough, especially since we were merely acquaintances. You can wave between classes. Sacrificing my room and not staying with all the other freshman athletes was a *big* mistake. I am not saying rooming with someone you know from high school *will not* work–but I would challenge you to live on your own and make your own friends instead of using a safety net, as I admittedly did freshman year. Have confidence not only in yourself, but also in school administrators to assist with living arrangements and to make those types of decisions for you.

In general, I was barely in the room. My typical day consisted of morning classes, afternoon diving practices, eating dinners with the team, heading to the library, and then finally circling back to the dorm. I was in the room to sleep and get dressed.

My roommate Jenn thought four roommates were simply just four too many. Plots and plans were made and laid to get Liz out. I do remember turning my head and not getting involved, although looking back, I wish I had stopped their plans and stuck up for her. These girls were cruel. I saw it from the beginning when boundary lines were being made. Meg and Jenn created lines with duct tape on the floor, declaring what portion of the 450 square foot room was their own, and we were forbidden to cross over it. Once someone claims their own space in such a tiny living area, the game is over. Additionally, once someone decides they only want a two-person bedroom when four people are supposed to live there, it is also over. Wisely, Liz moved out early–weeks after school started. I envy Liz's bravery to this day. Her confidence in taking the initiative and getting the hell out as she was victim to the bullying and ridiculous boundary lines is admirable. Once she moved out, the two remaining Terrible Roommates turned on me. Lies were told, sides were taken. And it only got worse from there.

I had difficulties adjusting to my new surroundings freshman year. I felt like I was in a tornado, buzzing around and being tossed out into various places and then picked back up to find my way. It was difficult juggling a challenging school schedule and an intense diving regimen, not to mention meeting new friends. I was homesick. I am a creature of habit and when an entirely new *life* had to be established, it was hard and scary. Freshman year IS an adjustment, but once you fight through the weirdness, it gets extraordinarily better.

One of the swimmers, Matt, had taken notice of me. Our relationship will be expounded upon shortly, but the more I stayed over at Matt's, the more envious my roommate Meg became. Initially it began with her teasing me, and then it evolved into more of her questioning me as to why I was staying there instead of our room. Finally in December, it just erupted and fell apart.

December 14, 1999

> TUESDAY 14 *This morning Meg was being loud and woke me. Up All day, Jenn and Meg talked to eachother, but not me. Then Megs friend-Hue called and I didn't know who he was, so Meg started crying and told me that he was upset that I didn't know who it was. So we are all having a meetin tomorrow about.*

This morning Meg was being loud and woke me up. All day, Jenn and Meg talked to each other but not me. Then Megs friend, Hue called and I didn't know who he was, so Meg started crying and told me that he was upset that I didn't know who it was so we are all having a meeting tomorrow about it.

One evening, the phone rang. I answered it and unfortunately did not have all of Meg's friends' names memorized and was scolded by her for this. At that moment, I should have checked out, requested a new roommate immediately. But I was hopeful it would all work out. Although I so badly wanted this newfound freedom, that same freedom did not include my parents standing behind me as they did all throughout high school. Back then, they called the shots, but now it was my turn. Truthfully, I did not want to give up on the roommate situation. It did not matter if I tried to repair the friendship–they had decided very early on that four people were four too many in the room, they wanted me out, and they did not hide their feelings about it. It was suddenly clear to me that I had to find my own voice, stand my own ground, and figure this out on my own.

Crystal, the Residence Assistant (RA), called for a roommate meeting. The three of us girls did not talk to each other anymore, more specifically, Jenn and Meg did not acknowledge me at all. Meg spread rumors about me, including that I "hung up the phone on her friends" (friends, plural), the kind of petty little bullshit stuff that others clung to. These girls were just *mean*. And now we were meeting with the RA, who suggested we find ways to talk things through and move forward as friends. That suggested conversation and plan of action never happened. They made it clear they did not want to be my friends, nor did they want me living with them. It was not until that meeting concluded that I realized people will not always like you for being you. The sooner you realize that, the better off you will be. I promise.

In general, please see yourself out of sticky roommate situations as quickly as they start (as Liz wisely did). You do not want to be associated with these people. Stay above the drama. Shame on you if you are the initiator. I wanted to try so hard to be at peace with *everyone*. Guess what? That was impossible. I spent too many nights worried about what would happen and hoping it would all work out. The roommate situation did not work out, and I turned out just fine, better, actually.

Letting a poor roommate situation determine your joy in college is a mistake. Letting a poor roommate situation cause you to *leave* college would be an even greater mistake. Get out of these situations as soon as you start to see the red flags to secure your happiness.

You do not need negative people in your life. You do not need creators of toxic environments in your life. Your life is way too short to allow for this. Clear your life of toxicity. It does not belong and only brings you down. It is never too late to make changes. Although it gets more difficult the older you get, and it is scary as hell, taking that leap is the best thing you will ever do. Further, find ways to protect your peace. And surround yourself with others who share the same interests.

I returned home for Christmas but did not spend much time in Chicago.

An amazing perk to being on the swimming and diving team was our yearly training trip. We went to various warm locations every Winter Break to "train." We trained incredibly hard! On our drinking… and diving, of course! We traveled to Ft. Lauderdale my freshman year, which brought so much anticipation and excitement. The divers went to one location as the swimmers' location never had a diving board. I roomed with my freshman teammate, Amanda. Amanda was from New York and rolled with the "cool crew." She was stunningly gorgeous with a petite frame, big blue eyes, and curly brown hair. She was always dressed in the trendiest clothes. Amanda introduced me to people I would have never hung out with–and I felt like a rockstar those nights. I was lucky to be friends with her. It is fun circling your way into different groups, even if briefly. I would highly recommend it.

December 31, 1999

I am going to go on a diet for 2000. So the whole team went out to dinner. We drank in our hotel room till 12, watched NYC, then Amanda and I walked around. We counted at least 110+ guys looking at us. We changed our names to Alecia and Julia, even though Amanda called me Mary a lot. To completely sum up the night, we were all wasted, we talked to more guys and got in more pictures than I ever have before. Amanda and I were thrown into the ocean, we rode on the back of a pickup truck, changed outfits, smooched off Budweiser. Amanda hooked up with someone and I pushed away a guy who wanted to hook up with me.

The Florida training trip fell over New Years. Our first night in Ft. Lauderdale was *so fun*. Our coach, Newell, took us out for dinner and then let us loose. I remember wearing this itsy-bitsy pink dress (helps that diving kept us in shape!) and walking around downtown Ft. Lauderdale seeing which bars we could get into. We had so much fun that night and returned to our hotel rooms shortly before sunrise.

I am thankful that while I was in college, we did not have social media to compare ourselves to the perfect girls plastered across any social media platform. I felt I was already under so much pressure to get the grades, be great at the sport, and to not gain the "freshman fifteen."

Women, especially, can easily get caught up scrolling through pictures of beautiful Instagram models who are a size zero. (There is nothing wrong with being a healthy size zero. I am just jealous of you). It really is amazing how much pressure is placed on women to look beautiful. Or fit. Or whatever look the general population has deemed as the status quo. I remember always comparing myself to other girls starting in high school. My hair was never as long and my stomach was never as flat. Social media can escalate this issue. One can either a) stop comparing themselves (which is very hard to practice) or b) do something about it. Doing something about it includes building your own confidence to know where you are at with your body is good enough. If you are on your own journey, stick with it. If you need to start your journey, focus on it rather than scrolling through social media feeds, which is simply wasting your time and decreasing your self-confidence.

After our training trip to Florida, I returned home to Chicago for a couple more weeks of winter break. As mentioned, I had previously babysat for a certain musician's son. Every year, there was a gathering of his friends and remarkably talented musicians who came together for a one-night concert. I always looked forward to attending the show.

January 15, 2000

SATURDAY 15 Tonight was Mr. Peterik's concert... It was so cool and sooo good. He had so many teelented musicians - especially a 17 yr old - Leslie hunt and a guitarist - Joel Holstra It was so good. He gave me inspiration. It reminded me of Banua - and I loved Banua~~ Music is what I want to do w/ my life.

Tonight was Mr. Peterik's concert... It was so cool and so good. he had so many talented musicians-especially a 17 yr old - Leslie Hunt and a guitarist - Joel [Hoekstra]. It was so good. He gave me inspiration. It reminded me of Banua - and I loved Banua - music is what I want to do w/ my life.

For reference, my high school ran Banua which was essentially a hodge-podge of comedic acts, bands, singing, and acting. During my senior year, my French teacher urged me, and then somewhat strong-armed me into trying out. I played one of my favorite classical piano pieces and was named an act. I truly could not believe it! The show was held towards the end of the school year. While three of my classmates played "Good Riddance (Time of Your Life)" by Green Day at the front of the stage, I was behind a giant green velvet curtain and took a seat at the grand piano. I tried calming my rapidly beating heart and wiped the sweat away from my hands. As soon as the guys strummed their last chords, the curtains opened and the bright spotlight shone on me. I wore a dazzling long black gown, which twinkled in the light, and let my fingers glide along the piano for the three minute and twenty-eight second piece entitled "Fountain in the Rain." I thoroughly enjoyed every second of every show. I certainly thanked my teacher for pressuring me to participate and wished I had done so the prior three years of high school.

I was certain the musicians up on stage that night at the concert had the same passion and love for music as I did. They had just figured it out, and I really wanted to do the same. I started writing my own songs, but nothing ever came of it. I just did not have the knowledge or access to anyone in the music industry to get me started.

Days after the concert, I was back on campus along with my Terrible Roommates. But things were looking up! I remember the excitement I had in January because my time with the Terrible Roommates abruptly came to an end.

January 24, 2000

JANUARY 24 THRU JANUARY 30

MONDAY 24 Today was great cuz at diving, I learned a 105B!! Yay! Monica did a 105c, and it was so good! So diving was awesome. But, the room situation sucks. Meg wrote that we are the worst ever roommates. Nice, right? And then when I got in from diving, Jenn and Meg were sitting on Jenn's bed. When I got in, Meg got up and left. Neither of them say hi or bye to me. I really hate them. I do and don't want to move out. I do - obviously, but it would be such a pain to move everything. We'll see - I hope everything works out...

TUESDAY 25 Its SNOWIN HERE! Our meet was cancelled today... yay!! Then I went to ORL, and they gave me a girl, Kat, who lives in Mckinney and I might move in w/ her. I would be a floor above Monica and Kate and by Melissa. So I am waiting for her to call back. I hope I can move in there. I really hate it in here. My roommates are psycho! But then I found out Meg, Bob's GF wants me to move in w/ her. I Also Excited To Leave. When I told Meg + Jenn, they were like "oh," and basically shrugged it off. I hate them & can't wait til tomorrow!! :D))

UGH meet

WEDNESDAY 26 Today was possibly the best Australia Day (Australia) day of my life! I moved out of Mckinney and into Mckinney w/ Meg-Bob's GF. Its so great here! I also got to get away from the bitches. Meg and Jenn got into a tight today about the Surge protectors. I really do hate them. Thank God I'm away from them. They didn't even ask to help and when I went back, they had already moved their shit into my closet and desk. Whatever.

Today was great cuz at diving, I learned a 105B!! Yay! Monica did a 105C, and it was so good! So diving was awesome. But, the room situation sucks. Meg wrote that we are the worst ever roommates. Nice, right? And then when I got in from diving, Jenn and Meg were sitting on Jenn's bed. When I got in, Meg got

14

up and left. Neither of them say hi or bye to me. I really hate them. I do and don't want to move it. I do — obviously, but it would be such a pain to move everything. We'll see — I hope everything works out...

January 25, 2000

It's snowin here! Our meet was cancelled today... yay! Then I went to ORL and they gave me a girl, Kat, who lives in McVinney and I might move in with her. I would be a floor above Monica and Kate and by Merissa. So I am waiting for her to call back. I hope I can move in there. I really hate it in here. My roommates are psychos!! But then I found out Meg, Bob's GF, wants me to move in w/ her! I am SO EXCITED TO LEAVE. When I told Meg & Jenn they were like "oh" and basically shrugged it off. I hate them & can't wait till tomorrow!!!

January 26, 2000

Today was possibly the best day of my life. I moved out of Meagher and into McVinney w/ Meg — Bob's GF. It's soo great here. I also got to get away from the bitches. Meg and I got into a fight today about the surge protectors. I really do hate them. Thank god I'm outta there. They didn't even ask to help and when I went back they had already moved their stuff into my closet and desk. Whatever.

A couple days into second semester, my friend Meg (not to be confused with Terrible Roommate Meg) grabbed me after English class as she knew I desperately wanted to move out of my room. I was almost in tears when she told me that her roommate did not return to school after first semester and asked if I could be her new roommate!

There is a long process involving paperwork, phone calls, and interviews with the Offices of Residence Life when switching rooms. I made the executive decision to bypass said visit(s) to the office, sprinted back to my room, grabbed a janitor's cart, and loaded up all of my belongings into the cart before the Offices of Residence Life could interrupt me. I had one hour to spare between English class and diving practice. There was no time to neatly pack up my belongings with bubble wrap. As quickly as Wonderful Meg asked me to move in with her, my belongings were tossed into that janitor's cart; time was of the essence. I was given a window and jumped through it. It was fight or flight. There was no thinking, just doing. My Terrible Roommates were toxic, and I needed out. I pushed that damn cart around my current building, up a hill into the new building. The problem was it had just snowed. Nothing was shoveled and the walkway was just slush. For every foot I pushed that cart, I slid back three feet. But I wish upon you the same determination I had that day. If you see something, get it, especially when there is a fire lit under you. I was miserable and could not wait to be freed. Pushing that cart up was my ticket to freedom and boy, did it feel good. I probably unpacked as quickly as I packed and everything finally felt right. I also thought if it looked like I was already settled, the Offices of Residence Life could not make me move again, right?

Wonderful Meg greeted me with open arms. We laughed, we smiled, and we were there for each other, just like roommates should be. We respected each other's space. We kept our areas neat. (When living in such small spaces, it is imperative to make an attempt to keep your room somewhat tidy). Wonderful Meg was *not* a Terrible Roommate. She was a remarkable friend who introduced me to six other girls, and we lived with each other during junior and senior years. I knew she was the opportunity I needed. And now I was living in the athletic dorm, where I should have been to start with. Had I waited for a call back from Residence Life, who knows what would have happened. In so far as my forty years on this earth have proved, *nothing* comes to those who wait. **You** make your own luck and your own happiness. It will not get done waiting on others. Although I have met people for whom luck and opportunity literally falls into their laps, it is a rarity. And should you be that fortunate, bless your soul.

January 27, 2000

THURSDAY 27 Today was awesome too. I got to go to diving and I got a care package. Meg is so nice - I have to get adjusted to this thing of talking! I also had a great piano practice. Then Merissa and I went over to Meagher and Meg and Jenn weren't there so I went into the room and got the surge protector and left a note saying Just getting MY surge protector. So tonight, Monica, Kate, Merissa and I ordered Golden Crust for celebration + me, I still need to pack, Merissa - I are gin to clubbies!!

Today was awesome too. I got to go to diving and I got a care package. Meg is so nice – I have to get adjusted to this thing of talking! I also had a great piano practice. Then Merissa and I went over to Meagher and Meg and Jenn weren't there so I went into the room and got the surge protector and left a note saying Just getting MY surge protector. So tonight, Monica, Kate, Merissa and I ordered Golden Crust for celebration for me. I still need to pack, and Merissa and I are going to Clubbies!

My second semester of freshman year had started way better than the first half. Rooming with Wonderful Meg was the fresh start I needed. She was a pretty girl from Massachusetts, with short brown hair and bangs. She was tall and skinny and sometimes cringed at my

Midwest accent when I was on the phone. She was just *so nice* and I thoroughly enjoyed her company. We would share a recap of our days when I returned from diving practices, or after she returned from a date with her boyfriend, Bob. It was as any rooming situation *should* be; I had just not experienced it yet and was so thankful.

I was also grateful for my strong developing friendships with Merissa, Monica, and Kate. We now lived in the same dorm, a floor apart from each other. Monica and Kate were roommates. Kate was a class act, a brilliant student and swimming teammate from Staten Island. Monica and Merissa were my diving teammates. Merissa was my best friend freshman year. She was a gymnast turned diver from a rural area in New Hampshire and the most naïve girl I have ever met. But she was so fun and carefree and just a *good person.* She always had a smile on her face. We had an instant bond, and our friendship grew from there. She was always there for me to talk to, vent to and cry to. She got me through really fun times and some really hard ones too.

The four of us became inseparable and were my co-conspirators when I retrieved my surge protector from the Terrible Roommates who claimed it as their own. It was my last crusade, and we celebrated our successful trip with pizza and beer. I was relieved to be done with those Terrible Roommates and never interacted with them again.

The diving season was quickly coming to an end. Every year, the goal was to improve the dives and qualify for the BIG EAST Conference. One can qualify by getting a certain time for swimming, or a score for diving, during the regular season. Qualifying for the BIG EAST was a goal I had made the day my parents dropped me off at PC. I had worked really hard on my dives and had finally qualified a few weeks prior! Not everyone on the team qualified, but I had made the cut and had to focus on perfecting the dives.

February 18, 2000

Newell woke me up by banging on the door. We practiced then dove right away — I beat 5 people. I was really happy with my dives. I got all 5's on my double. Then, 14 of us went out to TGI Fridays, Mrs. [redacted] & Matt came too. Then we went back to finals and Jenny Keim was sitting right next to us and she was wearing her Olympic ring and asked me if I had 2 elastics. And, psycho Merissa got the Miami guys autograph. We all came back on the bus. Tonight's our last night here. I just gave Matt a massage & I am sleeping over at his house tomorrow. Yay!

Today was the day! We took a bus from PC to New York a couple of days prior to the BIG EAST Conference. I was so nervous and equally excited. We stepped into the biggest aquatic center I had ever seen in my life. The smell of chlorine greeted us. We were allowed to practice a couple of times before the actual meet. I was in awe of the talent that surrounded me. We even competed against an Olympian! She placed first by over a hundred points and was mesmerizing to watch. She even asked me for a hair tie, and I gladly offered it while admiring her gold Olympic ring.

My goal for the BIG EAST was simply to not come in last place. I was excited to have met that goal and to have done quite well considering my nerves. The Miami and Notre Dame divers were especially exquisite. Every diver from those teams executed difficult dives perfectly. They were all tan, and their bodies were all rock solid without an ounce of fat. I had just never experienced competing against such competent divers and was astounded by the talent. Merissa strongly admired the Miami Men's Diving Team, and I cringed when she approached the guys and asked them for their autographs. But that was Merissa. She did not care what others thought of her and took home an autographed program signed by the Miami Men's Diving Team, which I am sure she cherishes to this day.

Sadly, the BIG EAST Conference also marked the end of the season. We took the bus back to PC, arrived at 1:00 a.m., and had one last swimming and diving team party. It was a bittersweet end to a great first year of diving in college.

Spring was upon us. The East Coast is very different from the Midwest in many regards; one example is the East Coast actually has four seasons. It gradually starts with a hot summer, moving as slowly as the leaves change, varying between dark forest greens to rustic reds mixed with bright yellows and vibrant oranges. And then as slowly as those leaves fall, the cold weather starts to creep in along with the snowfall that glistens when it lands on the beautiful, tall trees. The snow starts to melt, and there is so much green in the spring and as the temperatures warm, we welcome the hot sun again. Opposite of the Midwest, where it literally goes from a warm day in the seventies to snow the next day. There is no spring, either. The plants get confused and start budding while there is still snow on the ground and then one day it is back in the seventies again and summer returns.

In any case, all of us college kids were thrilled to be in the sun again and not bundled up in the cold. I flew home for Easter. Merissa joined me in Chicago as she had never been!

April 20, 2000

THURSDAY **20** I woke up @ 10 to go to the dentist.   Passover
Then when I got back, Matt w.a.s
online and he said that he misses
me. Mom drove Merissa and I to the mall
and we got makeovers and tried on
mermaid dresses ☺ then we went back
and dad made us these really good
fillets - such a good dinner. Then mom
drove us to DISNEY QUEST! It was so cool -
so many 3-D things- a rafting trip, a magic
carpet ride - 3-D roller coaster - and then
merissa and I did this drawing class - WE HAD FUN!

I woke up @ 10 to go to the dentist. Then when I got back Matt was online and he said that he misses me. Mom drove Merissa and I to the mall and we got makeovers and tried on mermaid dresses. Then we went back and dad made us these really good fillets – such a good dinner. Then Mom drove us to Disney Quest. It was so cool – so many 3-D things, a rafting trip, a magic carpet ride – 3-D roller coaster and then Merissa and I did this drawing class. We had fun!

I started my Easter Break at the dentist's office. My teeth were wrecked because apparently, the East Coast does not have fluoride in their water and the Midwest does, or so I was told. When I went to PC, my body went into some sort of shock and five of my teeth rotted out. This had nothing to do with the increased amount of alcohol consumed or forgetting to brush my teeth after all the shots, beer, and late-night food.

After the painful visit to the dentist, Merissa and I hit the town. I had so much fun being her tour guide that weekend; we ate the best Chicago-style pizza, attended a Disney Quest Expedition, and I showed her where I grew up, but not before getting makeup applications at the mall and trying on fancy dresses that we could never afford. We had so much fun up until she sat me down and told me she was leaving PC and headed to another college. I just remember being so *sad*. This was also before Facebook and Instagram and every other simple way of keeping in touch. We certainly made the most of our last month together at PC.

May 5, 2000

FRIDAY 5 Last day of classes!! Its so gorgeous out here. Then merissa and I played frisbee and then went over to the Quad cuz the Done w/ Civ thing was going on. Everyone was trashed and carrying around beer. Then we went to Ray and ate, got ready, and went to Louie's. it was so hot in there, so we went to Clubbies. I got so drunk that I walked to Matts alone. I'm lucky nothing happened. Then Sarah, Merissa, and Emily came to Matts to see if I was there. then I passed out.

Last day of classes! It's so gorgeous out here. Then Merissa and I played frisbee and then went over to the Quad cuz the Done w/ Civ thing was going on. Everyone was trashed and carrying around beer. Then we went to Ray and ate, got ready and went to Louie's – it was so hot in there, so we went to Clubbies. I got so drunk that I walked to Matt's alone. I'm lucky nothing happened. Then Sarah, Merissa and Emily came to Matt's to see if I was there and then I passed out.

Every year there was a huge celebration on the quad, not only to celebrate the end of school, but the fact that there was no more Western Civilization class for another year, unless you were a sophomore, and you would celebrate the true end of Western Civilization classes! We started drinking around 11:00 a.m. and continued throughout the day—and into the night. I had drank too much, left the bar without telling my friends, and headed straight to my boyfriend's off-campus house alone. While PC is a great school in a beautiful location, the off-campus houses were not in the safest areas, especially for a very intoxicated and vulnerable eighteen-year-old. I was so naïve! I thought I was invincible and knew everything. Thankfully, I had established really strong friendships after the roommate debacle, and my girl-friends walked together over to Matt's to ensure I was okay. It is so important to keep an eye out for each other!

2

FALLING IN LOVE

This chapter also begins at the start of freshman year, but focuses on relationships.

In addition to the initial roommate disaster, another mistake I made was falling for a guy named Dan prior to establishing myself at school and making some girlfriends first. We had met at college orientation and instantly fell for each other, something that had never happened to me before. He was intrigued that I was from Chicago and I was intrigued with his blue eyes, dimples, and East Coast accent. Many other girls were apparently interested in him as well.

Find your core friends first before falling for dimples.

September 9, 1999

THURSDAY 9 Today was 9/9/99 - just thought its cool. Today, Dan sat by this other girl, but then waited for me after class. Then Meaghan told me that he had lunch with 2 girls. Then he yelled @ me cuz I thought Bingo was @ 8 then he said he'd call me back & he never did. Anyways, I got this kickass care package. I got my laptop and a lot of other stuff. Kristin & I lugged it up here. It was quite interesting. My music class is pretty spiffy!! I had to sing - but thats okay. I actually understand 90% of everything going on. Then Merissa and I went diving. It was so fun. I can't wait to start. I want to go to the BIG EAST!

Today was 9/9/99 – just thought it's cool. Today, Dan sat by this other girl, but then waited for me after class. Then Meaghan told me that he had lunch with 2 girls. Then he yelled @ me cuz I thought Bingo was @ 8 then he said he'd call me back & he never did. Anyways, I got this kickass care package. I got my laptop and a lot of other stuff. Kristin & I lugged it up here. It was quite interesting! My music class is pretty spiffy!! I had to sing – but that's okay. I actually understand 90% of everything going on. Then Merissa and I went diving. It was so fun. I can't wait to start. I want to go to the BIG EAST!

When my parents dropped me off, they made it abundantly clear to me that I was there for school, diving, and music, in that order. But other things were distracting me–such as Dan. His accent could make any Midwesterner swoon. We had met during college orientation, held six weeks prior to school. Dan and I talked regularly on the phone that summer. We grew close rather quickly, and I wanted to introduce Dan to my parents before they started their long drive back to Chicago. As a reminder, I attended college over twenty years ago. I did not get a cell phone until my twenty-first birthday. We had phones in our room with a four-digit number that could be called by anyone else living on campus. When my parents met Dan, my dad immediately noticed his hand marked up with about sixteen other four-digit numbers. My dad pulled me aside and warned me of his other interests. I waved my dad off and foolishly thought Dan was solely interested in me. That certainly was not the case. My dad was merely trying to help, and I ignorantly tuned him out. It helps listening to people who give insight into things you *think* you know, but actually have no clue about. Dan was all over the place, but I never wanted to see it.

It sickens me that I actually *waited for him to call.* I don't know why, especially so early upon arrival to PC, I waited for anyone to call, let alone a guy I had just met. Maybe, stupidly, I felt at that moment, making Dan know he was my priority would make me his. Friends, this will never, *ever* happen. In turn, you only look like a pathetic, desperate girl. Do not be that girl. Be the confident, hot girl. Dan *never called.* Do not waste your time on people like this. If they are not giving you 110 percent of their attention, move on. This is even more crucial in your first few weeks of school. Start with finding friends. The rest will come later.

While I was still waiting for Dan to call, other things were happening that I was unaware of. Shots were being poured down my throat at the first official swimming and diving team party of the year, and while I was drowning in my sorrows, someone else was taking notice of me. And that someone else, a guy named Matt, ended up being a major part of my college life. Sometimes things happen when you are least paying attention. And maybe it is okay to not pay attention, but not for too long.

If I fell hard for Dan, I fell even harder for Matt. A tall swimmer's body with blue eyes. The butterflies were real, every day. Matt was two years older and incomparable to what I had ever seen in high school. Those boys looked nothing like Matt. We started flirting while attending our swimming and diving practices. I had the biggest crush on Matt and tried so hard to play it cool. Each week we grew closer and closer; one date a week turned into two and then three. He even started asking me to stay overnight at his house. I had never stayed over at a boyfriend's house before! I quickly fell in love with Matt because he made me feel safe, secure, and confident. Everything about him was perfect, except another girl, Heather, who always lingered around, sometimes too closely.

Matt lived off campus with two other roommates, Mike and Joe, who were also on the swimming team. Joe, a brilliant upperclassman, was studying to be a lawyer (and ultimately succeeded in that venue). He often threw valuable advice my way while we drank forties on their front porch. Notably, the boys had a pet chicken, named Cock-a-Doodle.

Matt's house was conveniently the central location for the swim team parties. I quickly earned my keep, cooking for him and his roommates, washing the floors, and doing his laundry. As even more of a bonus, I was able to do my laundry there too. He also had a car, an amazing luxury underclassmen did not have.

Matt was the solidity I needed in a chaotic environment. It was not easy navigating my way through an entirely different lifestyle. The new school, new friends, new places, people, roommates, teammates–everything in my life was entirely different, and having someone I could return to at the end of the day was comforting. The only slight issue was the guys could not come up with enough money to pay for the heat that fall and winter. It was *freezing* in their house and we were constantly wearing our winter coats during parties, while I was cooking and sleeping over. A picture from one of the parties somehow ended up in one of the boys' mothers' hands, and she asked why we were all wearing winter coats. "Oh, because we do not have any money to pay for the heat." Miraculously, someone paid the bill for the rest of the year, and we did not have to wear winter coats inside anymore! Funny how little you care about things like that when you are young.

Matt took me out to dinner in early October and as casually as one would ask to pass the salt and pepper, asked if I wanted to start dating. I almost choked on my food and did my very best to casually respond with a simple "Sure!" Internally, I was jumping up and down, but I had to keep it together. I was playing it cool, remember? This was the hottest guy on the team, and I did not want to scare him off. When the swimming and diving team discovered Matt and I were officially dating, I was swarmed with questions, including whether he had asked me to JRW. I had no idea what they were referring to. JRW is Junior Ring Weekend, celebrated junior year, where everyone gets dressed in formal wear and the class rings are received. It was discussed constantly amongst the juniors. I started getting included in conversations and was asked every day whether Matt asked me.

October 14, 1999

THURSDAY 14

Matt asked me to JRW! I am so excited. He came over this morning. I went to all my classes then and even did sorta well in singing. She said I have a beautiful voice. Yeah!

As casually as Matt had asked me to start dating him, it was the same circumstances for JRW. Someone must have told him, "Hey, you have to officially ask her."

He came over to my room one morning before class and simply asked, "Can you go to JRW?"

I shrugged and gave him a simple "Yes." As soon as he left for class, I jumped up and down with excitement and immediately called my mom. Guys must understand these events take much more planning on a girl's part than the guy's! Hair, makeup, and nail appointments had to be scheduled! And most importantly, I had to find a dress in less than a month! I was so excited and had so much to look forward to. I felt that nothing could come between our strong connection, and as soon as I reached that level of confidence, I quickly toppled over.

October 16, 1999

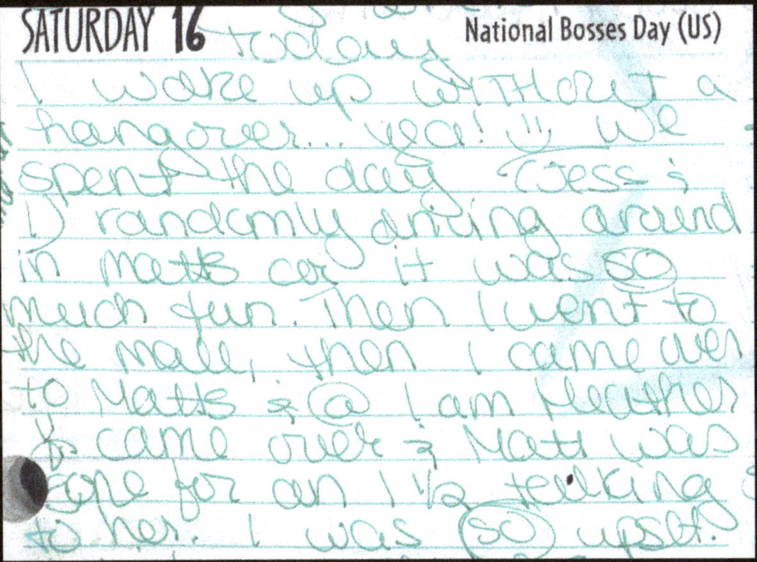

SATURDAY 16   National Bosses Day (US)

[handwritten journal entry]

Today I woke up without a hangover ... yea! We spent the day (Jess & I) randomly driving around in Matt's car. It was so much fun. Then I went to the mall, then I came over to Matt's & @ 1am Heather came over and Matt was gone for an 1 ½ hour talking to her. I was so upset.

Jess and Allie lived down the hall from me. I was closer with them than I was with my Terrible Roommates. Jess and I were two peas in a pod and just *clicked*. Allie was a blond-haired, blue-eyed babe who had a crush on Joe, Matt's roommate. All of us girls frequently hung out at Matt's and always had the best time, except when Heather interrupted our fun.

Heather was a junior, like Matt. She had short brown hair and big brown eyes that stared me down more times than I had liked. She was taller than me, and I was absolutely intimidated by her. She had known Matt much longer than I.

I was excited to be dating Matt and a little scared about how naturally our relationship progressed, so when Heather was literally knocking at his door (at one a.m.), some switch turned on inside me. I became fearful and resigned. I have never invited conflict or confrontation; I ran from it. I craft the best comebacks and arguments about a day after I process everything–but by then it is always too late. Even though I was Matt's girlfriend, I quickly shuffled to the sidelines when Heather came around.

That night we were all hanging out in the common room, sitting on the couches, drinking and laughing when Heather walked into Matt's house and asked to speak with him. Matt stood up and led her to the door and *left with Heather*. They were gone for almost two hours. While Jess and Allie shot concerning looks my way, we continued playing drinking games, pretending nothing was seriously bothering me. Matt returned, alone, and instead of flushing out the events and conversations they had, just continued drinking and ignored my needy eyes for further explanation. I simply did not know how to approach the situation, naïvely thought he managed it, assumed silence was confirmation that she would not be back, and tried my best to enjoy the rest of the night.

October 21, 1999

THURSDAY 21 Today was fantabulous. after music lab, Matt was there and we started talking, and I don't know what it was, but I just like him. so much. then I went to PC for diving and we had our meet, and I got 2nd place out of all the (5) divers! It was such a confidence booster- I ♥ diving. THEN, Matt called and a bunch of swimmers and I went to Clubbies- for the 1st time- It was so much fun. then we got back to Matts house, and I was so drunk I was talking to Cook. -darby

> Today was fantabulous. After music lab, Matt was there and we started talking, and I don't know what it was, but I just like him so much. Then I went to PC for diving and we had our meet and I got 2nd place out of all the 5 divers! It was such a confidence booster — I love diving. Then Matt called and a bunch of swimmers and I went to Clubbies for the first time — it was so much fun. Then we got back to Matt's house and I was so drunk I was talking to Cock-a-Doodle.

Matt and I were back on track. I was frequently hanging out with the upperclassmen on the team, which also helped me get into the bars with ease. I was also starting to find my ground with diving. My dives were improving every meet, as well as my confidence. I had even made friends with and conversed with Cock-a-Doodle.

Sometimes I wonder how swimming and diving is one sport. Albeit, we are in the water, but the only swimming involved on my end is from the diving board to the ladder. Swimming meets are very exciting and fast-paced. The gun sounds and eight swimmers shoot off the blocks, into the pool, and swim as fast as they possibly can. The crowd goes wild from that moment on. People are screaming at the tops of their lungs for their favorite swimmer. The sound of the rattling cowbell echoes in your ears. There are several things your eyes focus on during the intense race: the swimmers, the water splashing high in the air. Watching the swimmers' long arms stretch out and the final push at the end to touch the wall timer first. The race concludes, the winner is determined, and six more races proceed before the diving meet begins. Diving occurs in the middle of the swim meet. The aquatic center goes silent. You can hear the water sludging against the gutters. All eyes are on you. It is quite terrifying and sometimes overwhelming. I would frequently get lost in the zone, run through my dives, and breathe a sigh of relief once the meet was over. They are such opposite sporting events but are somehow combined. Matt frequently told me the "divers are the punters of the swimming team," meaning, as a punter will come in to kick a field goal during a football game, the divers were only good for part of the meet and could only score so many points.

But just watching the swimmers was cathartic for me. I simply could not help focusing on Matt and was in awe of his talent.

November 9, 1999

TUESDAY 9 I went to 1030 civ and music help and felt so much better afterwards. Then I just hung around till 3 then went to diving. I had the best practice ever. I am doing my 303's & 403's in the meet tomorrow! Then I went to Matts meet and basically studied the whole time. He came up to me during the meet and asked if I wanted to go out to dinner w/ him and his mom again! So we went to East Side Mario's...again. He was wearing his new gray sweater & looked so hot! I love him. But I won't tell him that till he says it first! Ahhh! ♡

I went to 1030 civ and music help and felt so much better afterwards. Then I just hung around till 3 then went to diving. I had the best practice ever. I am doing my 303's & 403's in the meet tomorrow! Then I went to Matt's meet and basically studied the whole time. He came up to me during the meet and asked if I wanted to go out to dinner w/ him and his mom again! So we went to East Side Mario's...again. He was wearing his new gray sweater & looked so hot. I love him. But I won't tell him that till he says it first! Ahhh!

My relationship with Matt was rapidly progressing. I had already met his parents and his younger brother. Matt's family did not live far from campus, so they were able to attend a lot of his meets. I also quickly fell in love with Matt, but would certainly wait for the day when he said it first. The last thing I wanted was to say or do anything to mess this up. I was too invested and in love with him.

November 13, 14, 1999

Then tonight was the formal. Matt looked hot in his tux. I got lots of pictures. The food was okay. I just felt awesome in that dress. I slept on Matt during the way back. I was so tired when I got to his house. We just had pizza then crashed.

This morning was the brunch. It was good... Flipi drove us there. Then we went back to Matt's house for a bit. Mike gave us a ride home and Nicole and I just got back from getting the pictures at CVS. They turned out awesome!!

All of us girls were counting down the days to JRW. I was so excited to have participated as a freshman! Nicole (Mike's girlfriend and a swimmer) and I went to the mall to get our hair and makeup done. I wore a long beige dress with a fitted embroidered top, halter straps, and a flowy bottom. It was stunning. I felt like a princess! I was so nervous, and Matt literally took my breath away when I saw him smiling in his tuxedo. It was surreal and so fairy-tale-like, all at once.

We danced the night away. I enjoyed every minute of the weekend and took as many pictures as I could without bothering Matt with it.

Twenty years ago, we took pictures with a wind-up disposable camera and had to wait for the film to develop. There was so much anticipation and excitement when Nicole and I picked up the photos. I could not wait to mail them home to share with my mom. Quite different than today's social media posts when everything is shared instantaneously. We were living in a different world and not one of instant gratification. Although difficult, I find it refreshing to live in the moment, instead of living behind your phone.

December 18-19, 1999

SATURDAY 18   **SUNDAY 19**

This weekend was so good. Matt has been so nice to me. He told me that he's everything he's ever wanted and that I make him "complete." He got me a really cute Banana Republic sweater. He liked all of his presents. I am studying for Soc[iology] a lot... I am nervous about it. Last night, the swim team showed up at Gravity. It was lots of fun. I had two gin & sprites and fries.

Matt and I exchanged Christmas presents. Matt gave me the confidence I needed about leaving him for a month, and I welcomed the Winter Break, but I was sure going to miss him. Sometimes it is beneficial to break up the routine and create some space. I felt like it strengthened and intensified our relationship, and those thoughts and feelings were validated upon my return.

January 18, 2000

TUESDAY 18 GO BACK TO SCHOOL I woke up at 5:15 and got ready. Then Mom drove me to the airport and I had so much stuff. So we got all settled. Then the flight wasn't long at all but I had to take a taxi cuz Matt didn't have a car. & then I unpacked, AND saw MATT! Merissa and I walked over there. We kissed A LOT, I ♡ him. Now I am back in the room cuz he is out w/ his brother but I am making lasagna for Reeder, monica, Kate, joe, nicole, mike, me, Matt & merissa! yay! Things in the room are shitty as usual... I am just not talking NEmore... it's not worth it!

I woke up at 5:15 and got ready. Then Mom drove me to the airport and I had so much stuff. So we got all settled. Then the flight wasn't long at all but I had to take a taxi cuz Matt didn't have a car. Then I unpacked and saw Matt! Merissa and I walked over there. We kissed A LOT, I love him. Now I am back in the room cuz he is out w/ his brother but I am making lasagna for Reeder, Monica, Kate, Joe, Nicole, Mike, Me, Matt & Merissa! Yay! Things in the room are shitty as usual... I am just not talking NEmore... it's not worth it!

The night before catching my flight, my mom and I made lasagna, froze it, and then packed it to serve to Matt, his roommates, and their girlfriends. I am sure it smelled lovely on the plane, but it sure was a treat for the guys; who doesn't love a home-cooked meal when you are in college? We demolished it quickly and then headed out to the bars to celebrate our return to school. Matt and I picked up right where we had left off, if not in an even better place.

February 6, 2000

SUNDAY **6** I went to Waitangi Day (New Zealand)
church w/ mom and dad,
then out to this Modern Diner.
It was good! Mom and I went
shopping "" and then they left."
I went over to Matts House
then and watched tv. then
Matt convinced me to stay
overnight there. so I did.
I like him so much.
so does mom + dad. This
week is gonna suck.

I went to church w/ Mom and Dad then out to this Modern Diner. It was good! Mom and I went shopping and then they left. I went over to Matt's house then and watched TV. Then Matt convinced me to stay overnight there. So I did. I like him so much. So does mom and dad. This week is going to suck.

In February, PC hosted the swimming and diving team Parent's Weekend. I always enjoyed when my parents came to visit me–they brought an unexplainable comfort every time.

My parents flew in to catch the meet and were being introduced to Matt for the first time. I think my nerves were centered around my parents meeting Matt because I nailed my dives. My parents offered to take us out to dinner afterwards to celebrate. I am not sure–between myself and Matt–who was more nervous, but the dinner could not have gone better! The conversations—and wine—flowed so naturally. My parents dropped us off at Matt's house in time for the swimming and diving party. I passed out at Matt's after the party but woke up early to make it back to my room with time to shower, dress, and pretend that I had stayed in my dorm room overnight. My parents arrived to see the new room and meet the Wonderful Meg before heading to church and taking me out to breakfast before they flew back home.

February 14, 2000

MONDAY 14   Valentine's Day (Canada, UK, US)

Today was AWESOME! First, my classes went by really fast and then at diving I did 2 105's w/out a call AND 2 303 B's without a call. Then Matt picked me up. We went to Chili's. It was so good! Then we talked about this weekend and then it was awkward. But it was awkward anymore when I walked into his room and Brandi ~ my new bear, was holding a rose and a card (which said Love, Matt) Then he drove me home. I love him so much!

I had never dated anyone like Matt nor had as strong of feelings for anyone else. We had yet to say the big L word to each other, but he *wrote* it, which made me think he would say it soon. He treated me to dinner and bought a stuffed bear holding a rose. I was head over heels in love with him. Nothing could come between us. Or so I thought.

March 2, 2000

I'm kinda mad. I don't know what to do — Merissa and I were swimming and she told me 1. That Matt's brother really didn't have a hockey game the night that he told me that he did. That pissed me off lots — so I can't trust Matt? 2. She told me that Mike and Matt play this game to see who can get the closest to hooking up w/ someone w/out hooking up w/ them, and I guess one night this girl started kissing Matt's neck... I am upset, but Merissa asked me not to say anything.

What the hell? I felt like I was hit by a train. How was this all happening, and how was I going to move on from this? Merissa was my best friend—as much as I wanted to, I could not run to Matt and question him. And truly, it did not matter, as it had already happened. I knew his brother played hockey, but every time I asked to go, Matt said no. My mind was racing. Were the hockey games a cover? His teammate Mike was also in a serious relationship, so how they both felt like this was a fun game disgusted me. Merissa had no reason to lie.

It took me a while to digest this, and I tried forgetting about it. That definitely did not work.

March 18, 2000

SATURDAY 18

He took me into his arms and apologized a lot. I also said I love him but he didn't say it back cuz he doesn't know if he does. Sunday: I woke up crying @ 7am. I told Matt 3 rules: 1. Respect me 2. Be honest with me and 3. No more talking to Heather.

The day prior to this journal entry was St. Patrick's Day. Merissa, our freshman teammates, and I partied at Clubbies to celebrate our Irish heritage. We were having a blast! Hours later, Merissa and I decided we wanted to dance so we headed to PrimeTime–another nearby bar. I walked in and saw Matt at the bar. I was so excited he was there! Merissa and I started walking through the crowded bar, and I suddenly stopped in my tracks. Heather was there–behind Matt with her arms draped around his neck. My face dropped at the same moment he spotted me. An eruption of anger hit my stomach. I turned around and pushed my way to the exit as Merissa witnessed what I had just seen. She quickly turned around too. We managed to squeeze our way through the crowd and escaped into the night. We did not talk; I was speechless. My strong buzz was gone. I was *mad*. We had walked about a block when someone grabbed my arm and spun me around. It was Matt. I could not even look at this man. I turned around and kept walking, and he stopped me again. He moved Merissa and I off to the side. I started crying–I could not find the words. He started apologizing but I did not want to hear it. He walked Merissa and I back to campus. She said I should go with Matt to talk. After all, she was right–Matt and I had not talked about the games him and Mike played at the bar. We had not talked about Heather–I thought she was long gone. There were many things that had to be talked about. I just felt so betrayed. I begrudgingly walked with him back to his house. I sat on the floor next to his bed and just sobbed. I loved this man and could not comprehend what was happening nor could I get rid of the visual of Heather so comfortably draped over his broad shoulders. I felt like the last five months were a lie. I had never experienced these feelings before.

And then he started apologizing. Profusely apologizing. He told me that he dated Heather before we met and that she could not get over him. He continued to say that he did not even know she was going to be at the bar and she had *just* joined him *right before* I got there. He further stated she meant nothing to him. Matt admitted when I was in the first dorm living with the Terrible Roommates, Heather lived there too, but on the floor below me. So, Matt would pay her a visit and then come up to the second floor to visit me. Cute, right? That newfound fact did not sit well nor did it help the situation.

Matt and I started talking in circles. We had both been drinking all day and the conversations fell flat. He begged me to stay at his house that night. I loved him *so much* and *could not bear* to lose him, so I stayed.

The next morning, I woke up crying. I was as equally sad as I was mad. I set three ground rules and naïvely thought everything would change. My foolishness was laughable.

March 23, 2000

> THURSDAY 23 So then we ♥ ♥♥ and then he held me in his arms, looked at me, and then said, "I LOVE YOU, MARY." I was so happy, and then I said it back. It was so awesome.

So then he held me in his arms, looked at me and then said, "I LOVE YOU, MARY." I was so happy, and then I said it back. It was so awesome.

Matt told me he loved me! Whether or not he really meant it, as soon as he said the words, I forgot about everything else and completely embraced his love–until the following evening.

March 24, 2000

> FRIDAY 24 Well, last night after skating (painful ☹) and dinner, I went to call Meg on Matt's phone. I was playing with it, and I heard Heather on the answering machine saying "can you come over and help rearrange furniture?" So Matt walks in and he said, "what's wrong?" I sat him down and told him that he has to stop visiting Heather and talking to her or else I will break up with him, and he has to choose between making me happy or continuing to make me sad by talking to her. It really sucks and I am really pissed!

Well, last night after skating (painful) and dinner, I went to call Meg on Matt's phone. I was playin with it, and I heard

> Heather on the answering machine saying can you come over and help rearrange furniture? So Matt walks in and he said "what's wrong?" I sat him down and told him that he has to stop visiting Heather and talking to her or else I will break up with him and he has to choose between making me happy or continuing to make me sad by talking to her. It really sucks and I am really pissed.

Matt made giant efforts to regain my trust and love. I quickly fell for it and enjoyed the attention. He asked if I wanted to ice skate with him. I tried so hard to do the jumps and twists ice skaters do so effortlessly and landed on my ass too many times to count. Matt extended his hands to help me to my feet, and we skated the rest of the night. When we returned to his house, I thought I would call Meg to let her know I was again staying over at Matt's.

To note, the guys all shared a phone. If someone had left a voicemail, you had to either listen to the message or choose to bypass it to make an outgoing call. I did not live at this house and always bypassed the messages. This time, however, the message started playing and I lost it when I heard Heather's squirrely, high-pitched voice on the answering machine asking him when he could come over to help rearrange furniture.

While reading this entry for the first time in twenty years, it is utterly evident to me that Matt was certainly visiting and still in touch with Heather all throughout our relationship. It was NOT evident to me twenty years ago. Also, it was an entirely different world as we relied on answering machines. No seeing or reviewing missed calls or texts on a cell phone. No scrolling through social media and seeing pictures of people hanging out that maybe should not be hanging out. Matt's answering machine would have been tossed across the room if two other guys were not also using it. I made empty threats about breaking up with Matt, although at that time, there was no way I could possibly break up with him.

Ladies, friends, readers. I beg you. If you are aware that your person is hanging with someone else, be done. Throw that answering machine across the room and leave (if you have the twenty dollars to replace it, of course). I honestly, stupidly, remember thinking, *Why is this chick still calling my man?* Like, it was the first time it was happening. No, no. It was the first time I was *hearing* about it. Matt promised he was going to stop talking to Heather! And I remember the anger that coincided when he told me he was still very much in contact with her–both emotionally and physically in contact with her. It made me sick. I honestly thought Heather was a thing of the past.

I was so wrong.

And this is when the senseless, irrational part of me was born. Up to this point in my life, my relationships were truly all butterflies and roses. Nothing worried me. I did not have many cares. I was so naïve. But then things changed. This burning anger in the pit of my stomach started and it was an awful feeling. This man who I had fallen in love with was spending time with another woman and I had zero idea about it. I continued in our relationship even though it ate at me every minute. When we were apart, I started wondering what he was doing. Not just thinking about him–but really thinking about whether he was hanging out with Heather. Looking back, as much as I was in the moment, it just was not worth it. But I really did think it all was. If it does not *feel* right, it isn't. Do not try to make it happen. It just won't.

March 29, 2000

Today was pretty mellow again. I hate 8:30 classes! Merissa and I got to take Matt's car to go tanning and we dropped my dress off to be pressed. Then we went back to Matt's and we all went to Gravity. Merissa got so drunk that she almost knocked the table over twice and she spilled beer on Matt and she asked Joe to BDB even though she already has a date! She had a bad night. I stayed over at Matt's.

Oh, Merissa. BDB was the Blind Date Ball, which was in a couple of weeks. It was a dance held every spring where the girl would ask the boy to a dance, for a change. Merissa was pressured to ask Joe (Matt's roommate) as Matt was complaining that he would have no one to hang out with, since this was an event for freshmen and a poor junior had to accompany me. (Another warning sign I overlooked or dismissed. Pick one). But that night at the bar, Merissa was doing handstands. Wearing a skirt. By the time I realized what was happening and noticed a crowd staring at her, it was too late. She then spilled beer on Matt and his friends, so I decided it was best for us to leave.

Not to fret, Matt *did* find someone to hang out with at the Blind Date Ball. Sure enough, good ole Heather was there. I lost it when he put his arm around Heather for a picture. I allowed her to ruin my night.

I told Matt I was leaving, quickly gathered my belongings, and left. Thankfully he followed me out and we returned to his house in silence.

May 8, 2000

MONDAY 8

I am just exhausted right now. I'm ready for Civ, my head is tired. I am sick of the thought of Matt and I not being together over the summer. I want to see him, but I have finals and so does he. Nothing is looking good right now – in 2 weeks from today I WILL BE HOME. I'm so confused. College is just like one long camping trip where you meet so many people – including the love of your life, but then you have to leave it all and go home. Just the fact that our relationship will be better... or worse – kills me – and I don't know which side it will be. Matt knows my b-day wish is sticking together over the summer. Let's hope it comes true.

I do not know where the camping analogy came from, but it is pretty accurate! In college, you meet amazing people. You are out in the open, learning about yourself and also picking up some survival skills. And then the next year you return, but to different setups along with a little more experience and wisdom that you did not have the year prior.

I was just *so worried* about our relationship. Generally, being desperate does not help. Being scared and worried also does not help. As much as you try to control everything, you simply cannot. I had zero confidence, and Heather had home field advantage. If anything, Matt should have been worried! But I was too committed and too in love to go home and enjoy my summer. I kept my head down and thought of Matt *way* too much.

May 12, 2000

Today was one of the best days ever, and definitely the best bday. At 12am, Matt called saying Happy B-day, and I love you. Then Kathy called @ 1 (12 Chicago time) and said Happy Bday. Then @ 11ish, Matt came over with a dozen roses! He also gave me Nomar, a stuffed animal dog. Then he brought me out to lunch and then he picked up the bday cake that mom had ordered! Then at night Meg and her parents took me out to dinner, and Meg left. I was bawling and then even more so about Matt. I went over to his house and watched all the guys play beer pong and slept over at Matt's.

Happy nineteenth birthday to me! The celebrations only got better each year. (Up until twenty-five, and then you freak out because you are closer to thirty, and after you turn thirty, you just feel *so old*). But back to the nineteenth birthday events. We celebrated by playing beer pong. When you essentially play the same thing every night or every weekend, you get pretty damn good at it. Beer pong was a serious collegiate event we very much excelled at. Matt would literally get *mad* at me if I did not sink the ball into each cup or god forbid, lost. We were all Division I college athletes, with major competitive genes instilled in us. This was serious, serious stuff. Smack talk, scary eye contact, and threats were always present and exchanged. Again, serious stuff. What was also scary was the basement we were playing in. Matt's off-campus house was built in the 1920s. The ceiling could have very well collapsed on us at any time. We swore we would all get asbestos after the ping pong ball or other objects hit the ceiling and a cloud of dust and debris fell into our beer. The floor was always sticky from beer spills. Cobwebs decorated the ceiling. It was not a place you would voluntarily hang out for too long. I think we were all just too drunk to care.

Sadly, my birthday was the last hurrah. Finals were over. My friends lived on the East Coast and drove home after the birthday celebrations. I was dreading these last few days before returning home.

May 16, 2000

TUESDAY 16 All my friends left today. I had a doctors appt. for the drug test at 11:15 and then when they got packed up, took my last final and then said bye to everyone. It was really sad but I hardly cried. Then we went onto Thayer street w/ Meg a my friend. We went out to lunch n shopped a little. Then Matt picked me up and I did laundry over there. Then Joe, Matt, Dan, ?, Mike and I all drank 40's. Joe & I talked about our future in law up on the porch. I really enjoyed it. Then @ 1am Matt and I went to bed.

All my friends left today. I had a doctors appt for the drug test at 11:15 and then when I got back I took my last final and then said bye to everyone. It was really sad but I hardly cried... Then I went onto Thayer Street with Meg and her boyfriend, we went out to lunch and shopped a little. Then Matt picked me up and I did laundry over there. Then Joe, Matt, Dan Tower, Mike and I all drank 40's. Joe and I talked about our future in law up on the porch. I really enjoyed it. Then at 1am, Matt and I went to bed.

I was thoroughly enjoying my freedom and the college life I had created for myself. Soon I would be working as a summer intern in a law office, where I learned life skills I still value to this day. My parents had also advised me that whatever money I made over the summer would be my spending money in the coming year. While making money and gaining experience was certainly the motivation, organizing client files in a storage room for eight hours a day under the flickering neon lights at a law office, instead of partying with my friends, was not. But I had accepted this job at the law firm as becoming a lawyer was currently *the* goal, and working at this prestigious office was a step in the right direction.

It was also fitting that I ended my freshman year right where it all started–on Matt's front porch where the first swimming and diving team party occurred. Please do not envision a sprawling, beautiful porch. This was the tiniest porch with rotting boards, littered with beer cans from weeks prior and cigarette butts shoved in the corners. Two folding chairs could fit, squeezed next to each other, and somehow, we had ten other wobbly chairs on the porch at any given time. But that was the house where I spent my freshman year, which had a great people-watching porch, and in college, you do not care about the sustainability of porches. You are just happy to be sitting on one. With a forty.

Freshman year was over. It was a blur. It was difficult finding my footing, balancing athletics and academics, and finding my real friends. There was (surprisingly) some homesickness first semester. Dealing with Terrible Roommates was not fun, either. But I focused on the positives: made it through, kept my grades up, made great friends, and learned new dives. Making Matt my priority when I was just an option was a mistake. I should have made my girlfriends and school my priority, and whatever happened with Matt to follow. Always keep the important priorities in order and the rest will work itself out.

I survived on my own after being so guarded.

And I could not wait for sophomore year to start.

SOPHOMORE YEAR

3

PARTY TIME

Sophomore year was the best year.

There was an unlimited amount of fun and laughter all year long. Many lifelong friendships were made. I excelled in school and dove in the BIG EAST Conference. I was in a solid relationship with a senior. I simply could not wait to return to school and move into the dorm with my new roommates, Sarah and Ellen.

Sarah was an elegant hippie with long, sandy brown hair and big hazel eyes. She was also an athlete–on the track and field team. It was nice having a roommate who understood the importance of balancing school and social time.

Ellen was an eccentric girl from a large Irish Catholic family, some of whom also attended PC. I had never encountered anyone like her before, and I mean that in the most complimentary way. She was taller than me and had shoulder-length brown hair, brown eyes, with a thin face and radiant smile. She never let anything bother her or did an impeccable job of hiding it. She was always confident and frequently laughed things off. Ellen brought the balance we needed in our room as well as the laughs and chaotic confusion. She was the friend who pushed you just that little bit too far outside of your comfort level and afterwards, you never regretted it.

I was lucky to have Ellen and Sarah as my roommates.

How three girls shared approximately a 475 square foot space is beyond me, but at that point, we felt we had the most favorable room.

Ellen, Sarah, and I quickly settled into our new space. There were two bunk beds across the east wall, situated between our desks. I had the bottom bunk; Ellen called for the top. The windows lined the back wall which had a ledge in front, canvassed with our favorite pictures in cute flowery frames. Sarah's bed was in the northwest corner, next to the tiny sink. The west side of the room held our three small closets.

There is always something invigorating about a fresh start too. Our belongings had their new places. Everything was clean and tidy–it only took a week to mess that up.

August 30, 2000

WEDNESDAY 30

I woke up at noon. I unpacked a lot more and then Sarah and I decided to go out on the roof. We were out there for no more than 30 seconds when a security guard came and yelled, Sarah literally dove back in the room. Then Kira, Sarah and I walked to Newport cremery. I didn't see Matt today, but he called.

I woke up at noon. I unpacked a lot more and then Sarah and I decided to go out on the roof. We were out there for no more than 30 seconds when a security guard came and yelled. Sarah literally dove back in the room. Then Kira, Sarah and

> I walked to Newport Creamery. I didn't see Matt today but he called.

Sarah and I were allowed to move in early as athletes started practicing prior to the start of school. We had secured the one room on campus that had a "balcony" and wasted no time exploring it. We opened our window, which was right next to my desk. We had to stand on my chair to step outside onto the ten by ten flat piece of roof, overlooking a main walkway on campus. We had a very quick adrenaline rush until a security guard spotted us. He yelled and started sprinting like a bear charging for his prey. Sarah literally dove through the open window while I waved "sorry" and casually stepped back into the room. Our stomachs hurt from the laughter, and we kept laughing throughout the night when we shared the story with others.

Being on the roof was the "haha look at what we are doing" moment. We were young and made stupid decisions without thinking it through. But we had successfully enjoyed our adventure, albeit for thirty seconds, and it was the highlight of our day!

August 31, 2000

> **31 THURSDAY**
>
> Today was so cool. Jill came down to our room when I got back from my run and she asked if I would go to Jimmy Buffett with her. So Sarah let me borrow her Hawaiian dress, Jill =. I looked awesome. We got their, found 22nd row tix for $50, and drank free alcohol before the show at the tents. The concert itself rocked, and I was so drunk! It was awesome!!

> Today was so cool. Jill came down to our room when I got back from my fun and she asked if I would go to Jimmy Buffett with her. So Sarah let me borrow her Hawaiian dress. Jill & I looked awesome. We got [there] found 22nd row tickets for $50 and drank free alcohol before the show at the tents. The concert itself rocked and I was so drunk. It was awesome!

Jill was Merissa's good friend and a member of the track and field team. She had just finished her run and stopped by as our door was open. I could not turn down an invitation to see Jimmy Buffett! Live music was certainly my passion. In about an hour's time, I borrowed Sarah's very cute Hawaiian dress, gathered water bottles to fill with our drinks, and headed out. And what else was I going to do on a Thursday night? We pulled into the parking lot and started drinking our water bottles filled with vodka and Kool-Aid. I think we had five or six in total and those quickly ran out, hours before the concert even started. Jill and I then ventured around the parking lot and were essentially cat-called by a bunch of Boston firefighters who offered us free food and beer. We decided it was in our best interest to join that party! It was incredible. They had an air-conditioned camper with a bathroom (which beat the port-a-potty in ninety degree heat). We filled up on all the food and liquor needed. They also conveniently had two extra tickets, within spitting distance of Jimmy Buffett. The "lawn" area consisted of sand. We danced all night and had an unforgettable time. The concert, from what I remember, was spectacular. And so were those firefighters.

At the start of sophomore year, I encountered other circumstances that clashed with what I had known my entire life. The first dealt with my Chicago accent and the second was wardrobe issues.

During music class, the teacher asked a question which I knew the answer to. I was prepared to answer "E flat." Problem was, being from Chicago causes one to have a strong accent with really hard A's. So, I raised my hand, was called on, and answered the question "E Flat." Although it came out as E Flaaaet, annunciation on the A. Twenty-two heads spun around so quickly and stared at me. My face turned red, I looked down, and never answered another question in music class. I was teased many times but remained proud of my Chicago accent.

I also encountered wardrobe issues. In my opinion, I found people on the East Coast dressed much nicer than those in the Midwest. Whenever I came home for breaks and my sister and I headed out to the bars, she always questioned why I was so dressed up, but I had thought nothing of it–that was the standard "dressy" look I had conformed to being on the East Coast. Further, I was grateful to be an athlete, as some days it was okay to wear sweatpants to class, but certainly not *every* day. These and other fashion rules were explained to me within days upon my arrival out East.

Another wardrobe issue I encountered concerned tube socks. When I attended a private high school in Chicago, I wore white tube socks pulled up to almost my knees, every single day. I continued wearing them when I arrived out East. I was on campus for Urban Action–a volunteer group who cleaned up various parts of the city. I put on my socks and was wearing shorts on this hot summer day–like every other day. *The looks I got…* You know that feeling when everyone is looking at you? I just could not figure out why and thought it was just nerves as I really did not know anyone. Finally, halfway through the day, a girl named Lindsay approached me and said "My grandpa wears those socks." I looked around and only then realized everyone was wearing ankle socks. I quickly ditched the tube socks and have never worn them again.

October 16, 2000

I am so sick today. I think it's cuz of the medication that I am on for that stupid allergy thing. Then at practice we all had to get into the pool with our clothes on for pictures. I was freezing. Matt called. He's being nice. I just hope I am better tomorrow cuz I feel like shit! I have a huge history test tomorrow. Mom and Dad gave me their sympathy.

My parents informed me that any money I made over the summer would be my spending money the following year. While I was grateful for the experience at a law firm, working for three months did not yield a high return of spending money during sophomore *year*. I essentially had to count my net proceeds and divide it by ten months, leaving me with about twenty-five dollars a week. That money would pay for any new clothes, beer, and late-night pizza. So, when an opportunity was presented to make $250, I was all ears. Some brilliant person taped a piece of paper in every single public women's washroom throughout campus about participating in an allergy study. I have always had

allergies and thought I would give this "study" a shot. Before partici-
pating in these "studies," ensure it is backed by some association. This
one was not. Ensure you are being seen by top-notch doctors or nurses.
I was not. It was the sketchiest research study. They assured me I was
on a placebo for allergy medication. I felt so strange and weird and
told my mom about it. She yelled at me—I felt like I almost heard
her screaming from Chicago. I got her message loud and clear. I just
stopped taking whatever they were giving me and asked my mom if I
should return the medicine? NO, THROW IT AWAY. So, I did—and
that was that. Oddly enough, and to solidify the sketchiness of this
"study," no one called to ask if I finished, where I was, or what was
happening. Be smart. Make sure you know *exactly* what you are putting in your mouth before you take part in this or other oral activities.

October 27, 2000

27 FRIDAY

I woke up drunk - that's always fun. I went to all my
classes and then no one but Adam went to diving. Then, all the
girls and I went to the Samson concert which rocked — then

Rusted Root. I was front row, center stage. They were incredible. I am absolutely fascinated with them. I got the lead singers guitar pic! I wanna be a rockstar!

Friends. Follow your heart. I may–or may not–have the paycheck I have now, but to this day, there is always that *what if.* Even at the young age of nineteen, I knew what was in my heart. And that was music.

Today I still get the same sensation at concerts. Getting swept away in the moment. Wishing I was behind the curtain, managing some amazing band. Organizing their schedule. Marketing them. But I had another voice behind another curtain (my father) who pushed me towards the more logical route. I took the *safe* route–the practical one.

Do me a favor and take the alternate route. The one that makes your heart skip a beat. The one you run to and get excited about. Because remember, this is *your* life, and you will be doing *that* job for the rest of your life. You have to start somewhere, right? So why not get your foot in the door at a young age and move up from there? I would speculate it is much easier than switching an entire career at the age of forty. While completely possible, there seem to be more outside factors playing a part in such vast career changes. Be the rockstar. Take the alternate route. And then figure out the rest later.

November 5, 2000

I have so much work this week!! I skipped practice to finish English then to start my papers. At night, Carolyn, Rob, Mike, Kelly, me and Matt went ice skating! It was soooo much fun. I got pictures. Then we went to Pizzeria Uno. It is so much fun to be with this crowd. I love Matt. He fell, too, and I didn't. Then we went back to his house.

Carolyn (who dated Rob) was a year older than me and therefore knew many more things about college than I. You know how you just immediately click with some people? That is Carolyn. We would just look at each other and smile and know whatever we were about to encounter would be the most fun.

Mike was Matt's roommate and best friend. His nickname was Psycho Mike, for good reason. Mike did everything spectacularly and on another level. He swam and dove on a Division I team without ever having attempted the sports, and excelled at them. He packed frozen food in his luggage for the training trips to ensure he would have something to eat. And if Outkast's song "Ms. Jackson" was played, you would hear Psycho Mike loud and clear belting out the chorus. He was just…psychotic. In a good way. He had a flashy smile, chiseled body, blond hair, and blue eyes and looked like the prince in any given Disney movie. You always knew when Psycho Mike was present as you couldn't *not* notice him or his theatrics.

In any case, Kelly (who now dated Psycho Mike) was a year younger than me. She was stunningly beautiful and invited me to the Jersey boardwalk where she lived with her dad during the summers, but I never made it out there and regret it to this day. If you ever get an invitation to go on an adventure, <u>take it</u>. You never know where it will lead you.

Carolyn, Kelly, and I became inseparable. It was very convenient, as their boyfriends were Matt's best friends too. The six of us regularly hung out, and if the boys were doing their own thing, us girls hung out. We created more drinking games than I will ever remember and always had each other's backs if our significant others were not as nice. I valued those friendships and remember having so much *fun* with them. Find your crew and hold onto those friendships.

November 30, 2000

30 THURSDAY

Today was awesome! I got a room - thanks to Sarah - who is pulling out ~ w/ Kristen, Dana, & Melessa. Practice went well, Matt is awesome, Then, I went to the BNL concert! It was UNBELICVABLE! It was so much fun. I wanna go to so many more. I love Ed Robertson!!! This weekend should be fun w/ Matt and Jeff. I'm so happy everything worked out.

> Today was awesome! I got a room – thanks to Sarah – who is pulling out – w/ Kristen, Dana & Melissa. Practice went well, Matt is awesome. Then, I went to the BNl concert! It was UNBELIEVABLE! It was so much fun. I wanna go to so many more. I love Ed Robertson! This weekend should be fun w/ Matt and URI. I'm so happy everything worked out.

I simply could not get enough live music while in college. I took every opportunity to go to whatever concert I could. Belting out the words and dancing with my girlfriends was truly one of my favorite memories. Take every advantage to indulge in the things you love while in college because it gets increasingly more difficult to do so.

While we were only a couple months into sophomore year, we had to choose our roommates for the following year. Thankfully, my Wonderful Roommate from freshman year, Meg, lived down the hall and we were still very close. She introduced me to the three other girls, Kristen, Dana and Melissa, and we decided to live in an on-campus apartment the following year. I was grateful roommate situations had fallen into place so much easier than freshman year.

December 13, 2000

> Civ went really well. I started to study for history but I just got so like panicky. I am really nervous about it. Sarah and I hung out in Ryan and Jay's room. They are real cool guys and that's it. Sarah told me that someone asked if I still had a boyfriend, but she won't tell me who – I am so pissed. I can't wait till tomorrow's oval!

Our dorm sophomore year was four stories tall with two long hallways on each side separated by the laundry room and stairwell. On one side of the hallway were all girls; on the other, guys. Ryan and Jay were roommates and lived down the hall. Ryan had short hair with an athletic build as he played lacrosse and wrestled in high school. He was the nicest person I had ever met. Jay was a blond-haired, blue-eyed kid from Massachusetts with an earring in his left ear. He always wore a backwards hat and was a master CD burner. Sarah and I would frequently hang out in their room and had more laughs than ever.

We were nearing finals and feeling the pressure.

The differences between going to college twenty years ago versus today are vast. Today, when one gets panicky, there are a plethora of prescription medications you can take to make everything better. And in certain instances, people who are properly diagnosed do very well with this medical attention. The problem arises when people like me, who have addictive personalities, think it is all right to pop a pill and keep going. What is scary is when people (again, me) pop pills when they have not been properly diagnosed with any condition. I was given a blue pill by a friend while in law school. "Here, it will help you study." It sure as hell did. I studied for sixteen hours straight and then crashed, hard. And then I *needed* another one. So, I masked the same condition that he had and magically received a prescription. Thankfully, that only lasted for three months before I returned home, and my primary physician refused to fill it as she had known me since "I was this tall" and knew that I did not suddenly contract any "conditions." The lesson to be learned is to be careful with what you are putting in your mouth. You may think "everyone else is doing it" or it will make you smarter, better, faster, or skinnier, but it definitely does not, especially if you have not been properly diagnosed. You are just slowly killing your brain, your creativity, and your health. Be smart. Be better.

December 15, 2000

Merissa and I hung out for most of the day. Then, we came back here and got ready for PrimeTime. I got wasted when I drank ½ bottle of 99 bananas. All the guys, Sarah, girls & me went to PT — I ran into a pole on the way there, went over to Matts and spent the night.

Merissa came into town to visit after her finals. I was so very excited to see her again, and we made the most of it. At this point, Sarah and I were regularly hanging out with Ryan and Jay. They introduced us to many new things which I had never experienced before, including 99 Bananas–which is a 99-proof banana liqueur. When mixed with orange juice, it becomes a delicious concoction. While Sarah, Ellen, and I went out on so many weekends together, no two were the same. They were all simply electrifying, especially after adding in 99 Bananas. Enjoy it while it lasts!

December 17, 2000

17 SUNDAY

last night was hilarious – Sarah and I banged for the 1st time. then the guys left the room, and so I went to bong it w/ Sarahs help – and it got all over my back & hair! It was so funny! I woke up @ 12 we all went to the mall, the pizeria uno. I didn't see matt at all today. I went to 9'o'clock mass and then wrapped up matts play-station 2 game. He's gonna love it. 2 MORE FINALS!!

Last night was hilarious – Sarah and I bonged for the 1st time. Then the guys left the room and so I went to bong it with Sarah's help – and it got all over my back & hair! It was so funny! I woke up at 12. We all went to the mall, then Pizzeria Uno. I didn't see Matt at all today. I went to 9 o'clock mass and then wrapped up Matt's play station 2 game. He's gonna love it. 2 more finals.

The most popular items bought at Home Depot while in college are a large funnel, vinyl tubing, and valves. Then, voilà, you have yourself a beer bong, which is the fastest way of getting drunk. Sarah and I were introduced to this contraption one night while hanging in Ryan and Jay's room. We observed them doing the beer bong with ease. And then their friends would come in to do a beer bong. They also did it with such ease! Sarah and I knew we needed to learn it–so we could do it, with ease. Said bong was hanging from the ceiling. The guys were called over to their friends' room down the hallway. This was it! This was our opportunity to try it, to learn it. Quickly. We grabbed a beer, filled up the funnel, held the valve. Dared each other to go first. I picked the short straw. We both took a deep breath, counted One. Two. Three. The beer plunged into my mouth. I tried swallowing faster than the beer was pouring into my mouth but was certainly not prepared for the wave of beer and Sarah's laughter as my eyes grew to the size of saucers. The beer exploded all over me; I quickly turned so it splashed all over my hair and down my back–at the same time Ryan and Jay returned to their room. Their mouths dropped open; Sarah and I erupted in laughter. We were filled with embarrassment and sprinted back to our room. And then resumed studying.

While the beer bong practices served as nice study breaks, I completed my finals without issue. I flew home for Christmas break knowing I would shortly be reunited with my teammates for our annual training trip and could not wait!

December 27, 2000

WEDNESDAY 27

The weather today sucked but we all still had a blast. We had diving, but I didn't do too much. Then we went out to dinner. I got real sad, and called Matt again– he had already called me today. Then we went to a club I got kicked out, then Emily, Amanda & I went in the ocean, skinny dipped in the pool then passed out! Drunk!

> The weather today sucked but we all still had a blast. We had diving but I didn't do too much. Then we went out to dinner. I got real sad, and called Matt again — he had already called me today. Then we went to a club. I got kicked out, then Emily, Amanda and I went in the ocean, skinny dipped in the pool, then passed out. Drunk!

Another year, another training trip in Ft. Lauderdale. Again, barely any diving occurred but a lot of drinking did. However, this year we were pros. We knew the lay of the land. We knew the bars, the restaurants, and the best beach spots. And of course, we reported daily to the pool and trained so very hard! The biggest disappointment this trip was getting kicked out of a bar. But Amanda, Emily, and I headed to the beach, found some more beer, and took a dip in the ocean. We had more fun on the beach talking to people and just hanging out. Besides the cooler weather, it was a successful and memorable trip. As all trips tend to do, this one went too quickly, and we returned to PC.

East Coast winters are pretty brutal. They are harder hit by the snow than the Midwest, but the Midwest always won with the wind. If my sister reported they had a couple of inches of snow in Chicago, you could usually guarantee the East Coast would get at least double that amount within thirty-six hours. We were in the dead middle of winter. Our tans from the training trip had faded, and I was knee-deep in schoolwork. I could start to see the light at the end of the tunnel for the Western Civilization two-year-long class that I needed to pass.

January 20, 2001

20 SATURDAY

Today rocked! At the meet, I got 2nd on both boards, only 6 pts from 1st!

Today rocked! At the meet, I got 2nd on both boards, only 6 points from first!

The end of the diving season was right around the corner and there was pressure to perfect dives so that I could qualify for BIG EAST; that was always the goal! I felt a mounting weight between school, diving, and my relationship. It was as if I was running on a treadmill with a ten incline, at top speed, with no break in sight.

February 8, 2001

So today a bomb was delivered for dad's courtroom cuz he is getting a bad case or something. I started crying, but Mom and Dad don't seem worried at all.

My father was a successful attorney and practiced law with his two brothers. He then departed the family law firm and went on his own before becoming a judge. New judges tend to be assigned to juvenile courts. He learned a lot in those first years and shared select stories with us. He even saved a baby from choking while the mother was testifying and proudly displayed the newspaper story in his chambers.

He was sitting in juvenile court during my sophomore year. He was assigned to some mobster case–or a case with mob ties–I am still not sure of the details, nor did my parents fill me in. Someone sent a bomb to the courthouse to inform my dad about the seriousness of this case and the need for a good ruling. The package was addressed directly to my dad and was handled while going through security before arriving at his chambers. A bomb squad was summoned, and officers escorted my dad out of the building. How my parents were so calm when they called was beyond me. I was not as calm and collected; in fact, I lost it. I guess since I was a thousand miles away, I felt too far and so afraid. Neither of my roommates were around–I needed to tell *someone*. I needed a hug. I ran down the hall and literally, none of my friends were in sight. Everyone was in class or out. I kept running, down to the guys' hallway, and thankfully, Ryan was in his room with his door open. "RYAN...my dad...," I said in between breaths and through tears.

Ryan gasped and half-jokingly said "Was sent a bomb?" The look on my face answered yes to his question and Ryan was both shocked and devastated by his guess. His face quickly turned into true concern. I cried. We hugged. Everything was fine. Why are things so much more dramatic when you are nineteen?

February 20, 2001

Today was the first warm day so I got to go running outside which put me in a real nice mood. Matt stopped over to drop off alcohol for the concert tomorrow night. He picked me up over his shoulder and tickled me lots and cuddled. He is awesome. Ellen knows Rob Hanssen the guy who was arrested today for being a spy – FBI guy for Russia. I feel so sorry for the family.

My roommate Ellen and I were getting ready for class one morning when her mom called. I picked up the phone and the tone in her voice immediately caught me off guard. She followed her mom's orders to turn on CNN right away. Ellen pointed to the TV and happily exclaimed, "There's Mr. Hanssen!" After we read the title at the bottom about him being arrested for espionage, her expression and tone changed. She stared at the TV as they showed FBI agents entering and leaving the family's house. I was speechless and could only stare at Ellen. Her mom was still on the line. Everyone was silent. After the wave of shock passed through, she told me how they are very close friends with the family. The neighbors witnessed the FBI storm through the family home early in the morning with no warning. The chaos continued for hours. The house was completely turned upside down and left the family in shambles. After Ellen hung up the phone with her mom, she started calling her childhood friends. I sat next to Ellen for a good remainder of the day comforting her while she worked through the shock and tears.

It was a riveting day. You never know what is happening behind others' doors; be mindful of that. While this instance was an over-the-top historical moment in time, it is a general rule. You do not know what is happening to others, or what they are carrying, mentally. Be kind to others. Always.

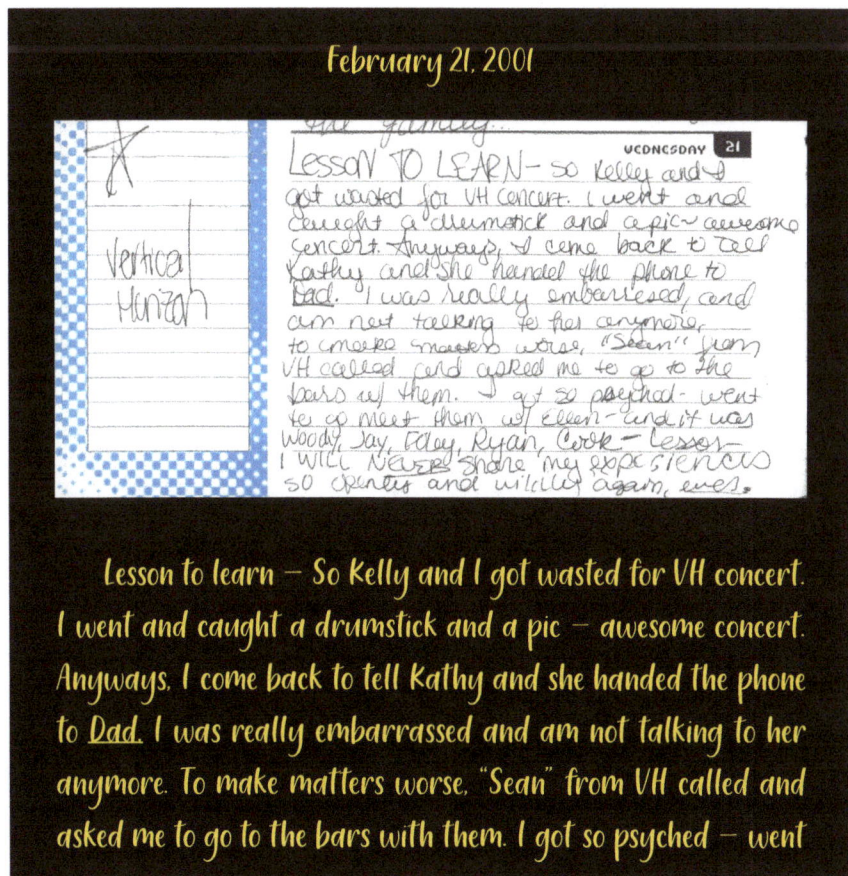

February 21, 2001

Lesson to learn – So Kelly and I got wasted for VH concert. I went and caught a drumstick and a pic – awesome concert. Anyways, I come back to tell Kathy and she handed the phone to _Dad_. I was really embarrassed and am not talking to her anymore. To make matters worse, "Sean" from VH called and asked me to go to the bars with them. I got so psyched – went

> *to go meet them w/ Ellen — and it was Woody, Jay, Foley, Ryan, Cook — lesson — I will never share my experiences so openly and wildly again, ever.*

Here is another life lesson—learn how to laugh at yourself. VH was Vertical Horizon. I have no idea how PC got such amazing acts to perform, but they did, and I enjoyed every single concert. My friend who worked in the college radio station knew how much I loved this band and invited me inside the studio while they were being interviewed prior to the show. I sat to the side in awe. I was amongst real rock stars and never wanted their interview to end.

Kelly and I got dolled up for the show, stood in the front row, and had an unforgettable time. When I returned to my dorm, I wanted to share the (drunken) excitement with my sister. I called her and while I was midsentence, *she passed the phone to my dad.* I was mortified. Remember the strict upbringing part? He had never seen me drunk. I was *wasted* and had to hold a real conversation with him. I was not prepared for this. I was doing great in school, with diving, and had a great front going. I hated my sister for completely killing my buzz and bringing me back to reality. (Do not worry, we probably started speaking again about a week later—this is just what siblings do). I quickly wrapped up the conversation and hung up the phone in complete terror.

What happened a few minutes later was even more horrifying. On campus, all dorm rooms had a telephone with a standard ring when someone calls dorm room to dorm room. It was a different ring when it was an outside caller. While Ellen was attempting to calm me down after that frightening conversation with my dad, the phone rang—differently—an outside caller! It was Sean from Vertical Horizon! Sean asked if I wanted to hang out with them since we had also hung out during the radio interview! Of *course* I wanted to hang out with them! Who would not want to hang out with rock stars? Ellen and I freshened up, grabbed our stuff, and sprinted down the hallway only to find

Ryan, Jay, and a bunch of other guys crowded against the hallway door with giant grins on their faces. They yelled "Gotcha!" and erupted in laughter. One of them had used their cell phone to call our dorm room and pretended to be Sean from Vertical Horizon. I was mortified.

Today, I still laugh about this. They really got me. But at the time I was completely embarrassed. I have learned throughout life you *have* to take things lightly. Let them go. Laugh at yourself. Never take things too seriously. Especially in today's world. Moments are fleeting. People forget about stuff. As big as things seem to you, they are not. I promise. You must move on. More importantly, never take anything personally. Keeping that stuff inside of you is toxic, and if you keep it inside of you long enough, *you* become toxic. Let it go.

March 4, 2001

4 SUNDAY

Its soo cool here —
we all laid out,
then went to Señor
Chico's — a sunrise
dinner overlooking
Puerto Vallerta!!
We then went to
Señor Frog's — I had
5 tequilla shots & 2
beers. I was soo
wasted, and mom &
dad were there!

It's soo cool here – we all laid out then went to Senor Chico's – a sunrise dinner overlooking Puerto Vallarta!! We then went to Senor Frogs – I had 5 tequila shots & 2 beers. I was so wasted and mom and dad were there!

Spring Break was upon us. I was lucky enough to go to Puerto Vallarta with my family–the whole gang was there: my dad, mom, brother, and sister. We had a sunset dinner overlooking the town; I wrote sunrise in my entry as I was still too drunk to know the difference. One of my dad's clients offered up their sprawling condominium to our family for the week. We gasped in awe walking onto the balcony that overlooked the ocean. We had chips, guacamole, and margaritas while we watched dolphins play in the water. Puerto Vallarta was stunning.

I also had my first *and* last taste of tequila during this memorable family vacation. My parents had dropped us kids off at Señor Frog's and said they would be back in a few hours. Unbeknownst to us, my parents simply went to the upstairs bar, ordered a couple margaritas, and sat back as the entertainment unfolded.

I cherished the time I had with my brother and sister and was excited to be hanging out with them. We wasted no time signing up for the establishment's scavenger hunt. The emcee sat atop the stage and invited participants to "go find a sock." The last person returning a sock to the emcee would be out, and the game continued until my sister and another girl were the two remaining contestants. The emcee announced, "Señor Frog says go find a condom." Our table was conveniently located at the front, near the stage. My sister and brother made eye contact and somehow agreed on a master plan; my brother, Denny, started fumbling in his wallet and told the other contestant he had a condom. She patiently waited with excitement while my sister actually *found* a condom from someone sitting at the bar, sprinted to the front of the stage, and was declared the winner while my brother threw his arms up into the air and apologized to the poor girl. The winner received *an hour* of free shots. I think I did all the shots within the first ten minutes. I was now warmed up and ready to dance! A handful of us girls made our way onto the stage and started dancing. Once my parents witnessed the emcee pouring tequila down my throat, they closed their tab and called it a night. My mother ordered me off the stage and ushered us out of the bar into the first available cab. The tequila did not last long inside of me. I found a new home back in the condo's bathroom, hugging the toilet. I remember my parents yelling at my siblings: "Look at her!"

And then my brother and sister asked, "Mary, did you have fun?" A big shake of my head yes followed by more puking answered their questions. It *was* fun; I just did not know how to handle my alcohol at my ripe young age, though I certainly *thought* I did. Actually, I did not really think of any repercussions from consuming that amount of tequila until my head was in the toilet. That was my tequila night. I vowed never to drink tequila again.

St. Patrick's Day, March 17, 2001

Today was so much fun – the St. Patrick's Day Challenge got me annihilated. Rob, Matt, Mike vs. me, Kelly and Carolyn. We only lost by one cup. I got really sick for a bit but Matt took care of me. I woke back up at 8 and just hung out. Matt and I are doing so well. I slept over and we went to East Sides for lunch. This afternoon was the first time I cried about the end of this year

What college St. Patrick's Day would be complete without a drinking challenge? The boys (Matt, Psycho Mike, and Rob) were paired up against us girls (Carolyn, Kelly, and myself) with one keg sitting between us. The challenge was who could drink more pitchers of beer first. Winner had extreme bragging rights. The guys were to drink six pitchers of beer, the girls, four. It was, in our eyes, a fair match. The only problem was Matt's younger brother was spiking our pitchers with vodka. Saying I was annihilated was an understatement. We had warmer weather that day, and I remember stumbling outside with Carolyn and Kelly, after we lost by one sad red solo cup. We started spinning in circles and giggling like drunk fools. Oh, but we were drunk fools! There was no hope for any other challenges or activities that day. I am wondering if age or wisdom or both–or something entirely else–has gotten in the way of my drinking habits.

In college, I just drank. It was so fun. Everyone was doing it. That is what we did. There were no thoughts of *I do not want to be hungover.* Or, *I need to be alert for practice tomorrow.* Maybe this is partially due to the fact I barely got hungover. Today, I barely even drink during the work week as it really interferes with the next day, and I am surely not jumping on the Peloton bike after that glass of wine. Oh, how things have changed! Sometimes I wish I could just *enjoy* the present– not worry about what is happening tomorrow. A majority of the time in college, I lived entirely in the moment. Fast forward twenty years, and I really wish sometimes I could just *be.* To not worry about what is tomorrow—what bills need to be paid, scheduling, planning. It is a daily struggle and constant challenge to be in that mindset. I would imagine anyone who lives in that mindset may just be a little happier and more carefree. It is enjoyable practicing that mentality and is most definitely liberating. Try it. Personally, I need to practice it more!

March 20, 2001

Rough day – I went to this law meeting and it was a shocker. Yea, I still love law, but the work… and they said that where you go to law school should be where you live – I can't decide that yet!! Then mom was like Dad & I are moving to Florida in 10 years – it just feels like I don't have roots anymore. Anyways, Ellen and I stood on our desks today and blasted music and dropped her CD behind my desk and laughed & went out on our porch. I love college!

PC held a seminar for students who may want to pursue a career in the legal field after college. They brought in a local attorney who had attended PC and explained that he majored in political science but also discussed other majors that were comparable and would aid in an education geared towards law school. He also described the type of law he was practicing, the steps he took to become an attorney, and what obstacles he faced along the way, including, but not limited to, the incredible amount of reading, researching, and writing learned in his three years of law school. He said we should strongly consider attending law school in the same state we would practice law. I thought I was being proactive in attending this meeting. To say I felt overwhelmed would be an understatement. It was complete information overload. I was surely not ready to choose where I wanted to live and study law while in my second year of *college*. I am sure some very wise students have figured this out, but I also feel greatly comfortable in saying that "not many" is an appropriate answer.

If you are like I was twenty years ago and not entirely sure what major you should declare, please know *it is okay.* My suggestion would be taking classes under the same umbrella as the field you would like to study. If I had followed my own advice, I probably would have majored in music (instead of minoring in it) and taken marketing or business courses to understand how companies run so that I would have *some* knowledge or connections to work as an intern or executive assistant at a production company or record label.

Generally, not knowing *exactly* what you want to do is also okay, as long as you are taking steps to actually figure it out.

As you move along in life, you will certainly see, if you have not already, you can be the most organized person in the entire world and outside events will bump you off course. It is really *how* you react to those situations that strengthens your character. For example, I did end up going to law school (and hating it) for one year, in Michigan. Did I have to live in Michigan upon completion of law school? Nope. All of my friends went back to their hometowns. Did my parents move to Florida and uproot me? No, again. They are still in Illinois. The things that I was So Worried About *never happened.* And that is my point. You are wasting your time worrying about things that have not happened or that probably will not happen. I know it is way easier said than done, but stop worrying! It does no good. A few years ago, I read

"90 percent of what we worry about never comes to fruition." Can someone make that into a magnet and send it to me?

My mind was completely exhausted trying to plan out my life when I did not even know what I was planning. I needed an escape! I convinced my friends to head north and ski for the weekend. They all quickly agreed.

March 25, 2001

25 SUNDAY

We all woke up @ 7:30 and headed out at 9. We skiled all day and it was beautiful weather in the afternoon. I had sooo much fun, and I feel that my relationship with Matt has intensified so much for the better. No one wented to leave, and everyone is so sore. No one got hurt, but now I have a cold.

We all woke up at 7:30 and headed out at 9. We skied all day and it was beautiful weather in the afternoon. I had soo much fun and I feel that my relationship with Matt has intensified so much for the better. No one wanted to leave, and everyone is so sore. No one got hurt, but now I have a cold.

In March of my sophomore year, the six of us headed up to Killington, Vermont–Matt, Rob, Carolyn, Mike, Kelly, and myself. It was an amazing weekend filled with skiing, alcohol, snow tubing, hot tubs, and playing cards (in that order). As it always goes, the weekend went by way too quickly. But it was a perfect weekend getaway and really the first time the six of us were able to travel outside of campus. No distractions, just the six of us kids, living our best lives in the beautiful Vermont mountains. The snow was fresh, the tallest trees surrounded us glistening with it, and the lodge we stayed at was a dream. It was clean and warm, and we comfortably slept atop fresh linens. We played cards around the warm fire and then once we felt brave (and drunk) enough, we ran outside to the hot tub to warm up our bodies and then ran back inside. It was just so refreshing getting off campus for the weekend and doing our own thing! Travel when you can. Go see the world. Do it all when you are young and before you are tied down to your spouse, partner, kids, work, weddings, and the million other reasons that will come up as you age. Explore! You will not regret it.

Another life lesson is finding joy or embracing excitement in your day-to-day life. This regularly occurred during my sophomore year, but even in present day, I try to tune in to the positives. You will start to find it is *easier* choosing joy than defeat. But surely, I had no problems embracing excitement!

April 2, 2001

MONDAY 2

Today could have been the best day of my life. First, Matt brought me over my fav kind of pizza, we cuddled, then had a v-ball game. I got mail today – from Vertical Horizon! An autographed picture! I was so psyched – I thanked the guys for playing that trick on me. Third, I got all my classes. How cool is that?! Then tonight I went over to Carolyn's and drank during the basketball game. Today rocked!

The sheer excitement and joy in this journal entry is the kind of feel-good energy I strive for daily. I encourage you to find the little things in life that bring you happiness and not allow yourself to focus on other minor nuisances. On this particular day, I skipped over to the mailroom and found a padded envelope addressed to me! I was astonished to find an autographed photograph from Vertical Horizon! After that very embarrassing night after their show, I thought, *What can make this all better?* I wrote a detailed letter to the band, telling them how I thought I was meeting them, when in actuality, I was met at the end of the hallway with utter embarrassment. I told them how miserable I was. They must have felt a grain of sympathy and sent me an autographed photo, which I still have to this day. It just goes to show you—you can always turn awful situations into something you will value for the rest of your life. I held on to the excitement and happiness for days after opening that package.

I continued my Exciting Day by drinking and watching our beloved basketball team compete in the NCAA Basketball Tournament! How fun it was to celebrate our school's team with my friends.

If you are not living your life and finding joy day in and day out, try changing your focus. Spruce up your routine. Celebrate the small victories.

Truthfully, I did not fully practice this mindset until 2016. My beloved sister-in-law, Michelle, passed away suddenly of a brain aneurysm. She left her husband and three small children behind. Michelle had no history or symptoms. She was simply on the phone with her mom one morning after the kids left for school and suddenly screamed in pain and dropped to the floor. Although her mom instantly called the police, it was too late. Our family was devastated and left in shambles.

We have all heard "tomorrow is never guaranteed" but until *that* day, I did not fully appreciate it. Michelle became our proof and intention to fully live and appreciate every day.

If you cannot pinpoint *anything* that will bring you daily happiness, start by smiling. It may sound silly, but I promise it goes a long way. Establishing a positive mindset and finding the little things that bring you joy will add up to long-term happiness.

April 25, 2001

> WEDNESDAY 25
>
> Today was great! Everyone was having problems w/ registering, but I got into my class fine/my schedule rocks :) I got a hair appt too for Matts formal :) Then at night, I played on a softball game! I pitched and played shortstop. It was so much fun. Sarah and I practiced the piano for our recital and then I watched Felicity at Carolyn's!

Today was great! Everyone was having problems registering but I got into my classes fine/my schedule rocks. I got a hair appointment for Matt's formal. Then at night, I played on a softball game! I pitched and played shortstop. It was so much fun. Then Sarah and I practiced the piano for our recital and then I watched Felicity at Carolyn's!

Every year in mid-spring, a date is set for students to log in and select their courses for the following year. It is stressful, exciting, and disappointing (if you do not get your classes)—all at once. Registering took no more than ten minutes but the anticipation and worry leading up to it was exhausting! Luckily, I secured my desired courses. By this stage in my collegiate career, I knew which teachers I wanted and which I did not. Talk to your upperclassmen. They have been selecting classes and experiencing more teachers than you have. Do not let them lead you in an unwanted direction, but hearing their input will give you invaluable information. Use their experience to your benefit!

May 13, 2001

13 SUNDAY

This is the beginning of having nothing hangin over my head for 4-months. People already started leaving! :) I hung out in Jay & Ryans room and we took a field trip to Slavin – I have no plans (:)

This is the beginning of having nothing hanging over my head for 4-months. People already started leaving. I hung out in Jay & Ryan's room and we took a field trip to Slavin – I have no plans.

Finals were over! School was over! Ah, to be young and free. I do not know how it feels not to have anything "hanging over my head for the next four months" but I am sure it would feel tremendous.

Currently at my age, this happens when I go on a "vacation" but all of the work I am leaving behind is still there waiting for me upon my return. Enjoy these periods of rest as they certainly do not last. And if you *can* make it last while pulling in a decent salary, then you need to share your wisdom.

4

FALLING OUT OF LOVE

MONDAY 28

Sophomore year, and still dating Matt. :)
I'm so happy to be writing
that! I am finally here again,
so excited to see everyone
when they all get here. It
was a 16-hour drive here. We
unloaded everything into those
bins, Emily, Sarah, and Bob helped.
It's so unorganized right now.
Then I went to Matt's, ♥♥♥ and
then Sarah helped me unpack.
Mom + Dad are going to Maine. CHEERS!!

Sophomore year, and still dating Matt. I'm so happy to be writing that! I am finally here again, so excited to see everyone when they all get here. It was a 16 hour drive here. We unloaded everything into those bins. Emily Sarah and Bob helped. It's so unorganized right now. Then I went to Matt's and then Sarah helped me unpack. Mom and Dad are going to Maine. Cheers!

September 8, 2000

> **8 FRIDAY**
> Tonight was awesome. we started at mikes, then went to Maggies, then Lori's. Psycho asked about sarah!! :) Then after we were all shit-faced - matt keith and I went to the Pig Roast and Ellen and I got in and drank more. then we went to Pat's house then Matts. ♥♥♥ Then I was so drunk that I told matt that he has my heart :) he told me too that he saw heather and looked away! :) Its done with her, completly.

Tonight was awesome. We started at Mike's, then went to Maggie's, then Lori's. Psycho asked about Sarah. Then after we were all shit-faced Matt, Keith and I went to the Pig Roast and Ellen and I got in and drank more. Then we went to Pat's house, then Matt's. Then I was so drunk that I told Matt that he has my heart. He told me too that he saw Heather and looked away. It's done with her completely.

Again circling back to the start of sophomore year, I had more confidence than I did freshman year and was so relieved to be back with Matt. We had successfully made our long-distance relationship work. I wrote letters and received a couple from him as well. We called each other frequently. We both traveled to each other's hometowns and enjoyed our time together. We picked right up where we left off. I felt like nothing could go wrong!

September 15, 2000

Today, Sarah & I went to practice and then Gravity. Matt & Mike were completely drunk cuz they drank 6 pitchers in 1.24:36. They were so drunk and Matt and I had a serious talk — he said that he really started loving me when he came out to Chicago, and he didn't think that it was going to last over the summer. It made me real sad, but I guess I should be happy cuz he definitely loves me now and nothing is artificial. I don't know — it makes me think a lot about the future & where I'll live... Nick sent me a song called Spend a Lifetime!

I was happy to see Matt at the bar, but I was not prepared for his confession. While it was difficult being away from him over the summer, I had fallen in love with Matt much earlier than he apparently had. I was also relieved we made it through the summer but did not realize he had reservations; he never shared them with me. Quite the opposite, he promised everything would be fine and told me not to worry.

It is never a wise idea to speak with someone about the status of your relationship after consuming that amount of alcohol in an hour and a half. Why I thought it was impeccable timing to do so is beyond me, but tread carefully and stick with the funny and light conversation after encountering people who have already consumed *that much beer.* You can thank me later.

October 2, 2000

Today I wore a pretty dress for our anniversary, and Matt came over and visited. I love him so much and if you are ever stupid enough to worry about anything anymore, then I am crazy cuz Matt bought me this beautiful ring and he wouldn't have if he didn't love me. He tho, is not feeling to well. Dan has mono on our team – I'm praying he doesn't.

In October, Matt and I celebrated our one-year anniversary. Matt bought me a stunning aquamarine ring. In hindsight, it reminds of comedian Ron White's more famous lines "Diamonds. That'll shut her up." Dear Ron White: it works. I legitimately thought the ring was a college version of the real deal; I took this relationship *that* seriously. But in actuality, the ring was nothing more than an anniversary present.

I was truly excited to still be with Matt, however, our relationship was really unbalanced. I was in–100 percent. I was faithful and dedicated. I would have dropped anything for Matt at any given time. But Matt had other interests. While I do not know whether he acted on those other interests, they were present, and he definitely did not do anything to stop them. This imbalance was a recipe for disaster.

I fully applaud high school/college sweethearts who have made it work. Cheers to you for somehow keeping sane and outside factors… outside. There was way too much noise for me and frankly, looking back, we were still just two young kids in love.

November 4, 2000

> 4 SATURDAY
>
> Today was excellent – 2nd place w/ diving, and no mistakes with my piece" Ellen ÷ I went to Hemenuoos w/ mom & dad. Last night, Matt & I played this "point" game- like who has done more for who – and I won – by a lot… it just got me upset… shouldn't he be winning?? " at Matt's tonight "

> Today was excellent – 2nd place with diving and no mistakes with my piece. Ellen and I went to Hemingway's with Mom and Dad. Last night, Matt and I played this "point" game – like who has done more for who – and I won – by a lot... it just got me upset... shouldn't he be winning?? At Matt's tonight.

I loved when my parents visited, and being treated to a fancy restaurant was always a fantastic surprise. Cafeteria food and ramen can only take you so far. Ellen and I were fed, dropped off at Matt's, and joined the party.

At this point, almost at the end of first semester in sophomore year, was about the time my relationship with Matt slowly started to deteriorate. There were a ton of outside factors encircling me, such as people suggesting I do too much for him and implications he took me for granted. Both were true but I did not want to see it, believe it, or hear any of it. Either way, I certainly was not ready to let go yet. And the harder I held on, the more emotional it was. I tried too hard to make it last.

Further, there should never be a "point" game in relationships. I had to win; I could not let Heather win. That is what my relationship was: a competition. The longer I held on, the harder it was for her to win. And it was during these moments when the deterioration began. I really do not know how the point game started. I most likely had too much to drink one night and started nagging Matt. We would take turns asking questions and the last to have done it got a point. The last to cook for the other? Me. The last to do the other's laundry? Me. The last one who did something nice for the other? Me again. The moment that you start playing point games in relationships, you should know that you are headed down a scary and unsure road. The moment that you are no longer "winning" or feeling that way, should be the same moment you choose a different path–and stop playing point games.

November 7, 2000

TUESDAY 7

Election Day – still – no winner is decided.
I have decided something, thanks to the
help of Nick – Matt never did anything
wrong to you. Both of us flirt = boost
of ego. Don't get mad. If you keep
it up, you won't be around – who
likes "worry wads"?? Leave it alone –
everything is grand. Look at your
freakin Hand – would he buy you
it if he had doubts about our
relationship?? Grow up Mary,   stop worrying
enjoy your relationship, and chill out.   too.

Election Day – still no winner is decided. I have decided
something, thanks to the help of Nick – Matt never did anything
wrong to you. Both of us flirt = boost of ego. Don't get mad.
If you keep it up, you won't be around – who likes "worry
wads"?? Leave it alone – everything is grand. Look at your
freakin hand – would he buy you it if he had doubts about our
relationship?? Grow up Mary, enjoy your relationship and chill
out. Stop worrying too.

Our dorm was seeking elected officials to represent the needs of
all residents and speak on their behalf. Wonderful Meg and I ran for
vice president and president, respectively, (and won)! I cannot stress
enough the importance of getting involved on campus–whether with
sports, clubs, or extracurriculars. I met wonderful like-minded leaders
while being President of Aquinas Hall, which also looked wonderful
on my resume! As much as my assurance was growing, I was really

starting to struggle with Matt. Additional outside factors also started creeping in.

Nick was one of those aforementioned outside factors (although I did not know that yet). Nick and I met through mutual friends the summer before college and spent time at Willow Pool, showing off our crazy dives and pretending to strictly be friends as he had a girlfriend. We could walk or rollerblade to each other's houses via the "black path" that ran between our neighborhoods. It was exactly what it was called–a black path with zero lighting. That summer was certainly memorable. My parents lifted the curfew, I was hanging out with Nick and his friends *all the time,* and was literally having the best summer. Halfway through the summer and before leaving for college, he sadly broke up with his girlfriend. We were more than friends but also could not commit to each other knowing we were going to be thousands of miles apart in just a few short weeks. So, we made the best of it. I was always smiling and laughing with him. If we were not showing off our dives at the pool, we were at the park at night swinging on swings, talking about our lives–our hopes and dreams and what we wanted to do with them. We had picnics on the black path, on his driveway, in his basement, everywhere away from our parents. We became very close in those summer months. And then we went away, onto our separate lives, without any closure.

We had kept in touch, and he was currently "helping" me figure out my emotions with Matt, all the while patiently sitting back and waiting for his opportunity to pounce. (Sneak peak, he did, and it was a disaster of my own doing). I was slowly starting to digest the fact that Matt was not my person. I thought he was and wanted him to be. However, there is certainly no reason to write mini pep talks for oneself while they are supposed to be having the best four years of their life.

December 2, 2000

I kicked ass on 3 meter! Matt was being nice at the meet too. We, (the divers), grabbed a really good lunch. After the meet, I came back, and Carolyn, Kelly and I drank, then went over to the guys house. I was so drunk. I had a blast!

December 18, 2000

I think that I aced English today. Dr. Lynch then came out
and told me to still consider being an English major... I went to
the mall w/ Carolyn, but I couldn't find a skirt for tomorrow
for Al Forno. I went out to dinner @ East Side Mario's with Matt.
I called him perfect and he said, 'part of that is being w/ you!'
He gave me aqua colored pajamas for Christmas.

I wrapped up finals and celebrated an early Christmas with Matt
before heading home for Christmas break. I was steadfastly holding
onto the good times with Matt, not knowing many more bad times
would outnumber the good times upon our return.

January 3, 2001

WEDNESDAY 3

So today sucked cuz I had to leave @ 1, so I got to the airport with 7 hours to waste!! Then, I bought a book about relationships and it really cleared up my head. I only read like 30 pages, but I learned that ① I feel resentment b/c I give a lot, and in turn, I don't always get back nurturing ② Matt needs to be appreciated and shown fulfillment in everything!! I feel sick 🙁 I don't wanna work!!

So today sucked cuz I had to leave at 1, so I got to the airport with 7 hours to waste. Then, I bought a book about relationships and it really cleared up my head. I only read like 30 pages, but I learned that 1. I feel resentment because I give a lot, and in turn, I don't always get back nurturing 2. Matt needs to be appreciated and shown fulfillment in everything. I feel sick. I don't wanna work.

Once you start relying on the self-help books at age nineteen for your college relationship, it is safe to say it is over. We all have our own minds, our own ways; we are our own beings. Please do not buy self-help books in order to mold yourself into a different human *for* another human. Do not be mistaken–I absolutely think self-help books work. They offer advice and insight on how to look at things differently and can open your mind to new ideas. I have read my fair share of these books. I just personally feel when you are nineteen-years-young and grasping onto self-help books *in college,* the relationship is over.

My problem was I took everything in that book literally and changed my mindset *for* Matt. *For* my sanity. *For* my relationship. I had to read a book to justify my actions. I really wanted to have a stable, happy, long-term relationship. I clung to the thought that *maybe it is me*. Really though, it was not me. We just were not meant to be. Sometimes you will be so distraught and so upset about a silly situation, and the sooner you realize "it is okay, it was not meant to be," the sooner you can reclaim your happiness and continue with your life. Especially when you are nineteen. Just BE.

January 19, 2001

19 FRIDAY

On the bus ride to Maine, Matt and I got in a stupid fight about his magazine cuz it got tape on it. And then he told me that I criticize him to much. So I was crying and he didn't come up to my room to talk, so I went down there and told him how much effort I put into the relationship and how easily he changes my feelings. So now I feel lots better, especially knowing that he knows how I feel.

I finally built up the courage to approach Matt to validate and share my feelings. I had everything bottled up and it felt amazing to let it out. I was also upset we were in a fight on our way up to Maine, for a meet. I wish I had been able to take my frustrations with Matt out on the diving board, but that never happened, and instead, I did not dive well. The amount of my time and energy this man wasted was excessive, and it only got worse.

January 23, 2001

Mike and Kelly broke up. Kelly is so sad. Carolyn and I were talking and she is just like me – like worrying and stuff. It's just that I freak out about breaking up. Tonight we went to Stuarts and made signs for the seniors. I walked over to Matt's house to surprise him and he wasn't there. He called it "weird." I have so much work. Divings almost done.

Carolyn and I were worried when Kelly and Mike broke up. First, they were the strongest couple between the three of us. Second, Psycho

Mike and Matt were best friends, and if Mike proved he had more fun being single, Matt was not hard to convince otherwise. The odds were starting to stack against me.

January 24, 2001

WEDNESDAY 24

Tonight, Matt took me out to Pizzeria Uno. Then he took me to a movie. He opened doors for me, put his arm around me, put on my jacket for me — it was a night that I would repeat forever. Then when we were pulling up to Aquinas (cuz I have a Civ quiz tomorrow) Psycho Mike and Co. walked up and were talking about Brads & Fish Co for tomorrow night. I got this pit in my stomach and I don't know why. I hate that! Why?! I need to stop doing that. Tonight rocked. I guess I just don't like the idea of Matt at bars?! help.

I felt Matt and I were back on track again. He made me feel loved and fulfilled. We had a delicious meal, watched a movie of my choice, and held hands in the car on the way back to my dorm. I was smiling from ear to ear and on cloud nine. I was just *so happy* being with this man.

And then his friends approached as we pulled into campus. They reminded him about their night out tomorrow at Fish Co. My smile disappeared and the ball of anger quickly returned to my stomach. It wasn't that I did not like the thought of Matt at bars. That pit in my stomach is called *intuition*. It is called–I knew there was a great possibility that Heather would be at that bar and I did not want her draping her arms over Matt again. Fish Co. was a bar Heather *always* hung out at and I could not get into said bar because they carded *hard*. I could not risk losing my beloved ID, and the thought of Matt hanging out with Heather while our relationship was starting to spiral made me sick.

These continuing bouts of worry and the pits in my stomach without any confirmation or confidence from Matt were devastating blows to our relationship. I wish I followed my gut more than I had. In all my years in this life, my gut has not been wrong. It has not misdirected me. It just *knows*. About half the time, I choose not to listen to it; I forge my own path and figure it out later, usually to my dismay. Following your gut will quickly take you to where you should be.

February 7, 2001

> WEDNESDAY 7
>
> I ran this morning—I am looking fwd to the summer when I can run everyday! Tonight I went to PrimeTime. Heather and PsychoMike were there together. Waves of anger passed thru me for the whole night. I can't believe Mike is playing so many girls at once. I got wasted cuz Kristen didn't want to leave, so I came back here w/ her & Ellen and Sarah yelled at us for being loud, so I went down to Jay's room and ended up passin out till 7:30! ☺

I ran this morning. I am looking forward to the summer when I can run everyday! Tonight I went to Prime Time. Heather and Psycho Mike were there together. Waves of anger passed thru me for the whole night. I can't believe Mike is playing so many girls at once. I got wasted cuz Kristen didn't want to leave. So I came back here with her & Ellen and Sarah yelled at us for being loud, so I went down to Jay's room and ended up passing out till 7:30!

I erupted in anger when I saw Matt's best friend with Heather. Whose side was he on? All in all, he is a very nice guy and a loyal friend. But he was Matt's best friend, not mine. It was not about sides, it was the fact that I was feeling threatened and in awe that he would be hanging out with Heather so soon after breaking up with Kelly.

Our relationship was unwinding. I was scared to let go of the one consistent factor I had in college. Every semester I had different classes, different classmates; while diving was consistent, our coach was not. He was (although a fantastic coach) barely there, and that worsened as the seasons continued. Matt was my home base. I was so lucky to have somewhere else to stay while going through the freshman year roommate debacle. And it was all slowly unwinding right in front of my eyes, and I did not know what to do or what life looked like without that safety net. But sometimes you just have to let go and not worry about what your new life looks like. As many changes as I have had during my life, waking up to new chapters and new challenges always made me a better, stronger, and most importantly, happier person.

February 14, 2001

WEDNESDAY 14

NT Possibly the best day of my life...matt picked me up at 6, and said let's exchange presents and then go to McDonalds. So we went into his house. He opened the bedroom door, and there was the table, w/ a red table cloth, 12 magenta roses, dinner (5 course) all set and ready to go, and most importantly a card, in which he wrote that "I have nothing to worry about, especially in Cancun" then there were heart-shaped sugar cookies... It was a perfect evening. We cuddled for like 4 hours, ♥♥, he had all the food ready, and his room was immaculate. He is the perfect guy, and gave me such a special night that I will never forget.

Possibly the best day of my life... Matt picked me up at 6 and said let's exchange presents and then go to McDonald's. So we went into his house. He opened the bedroom door and there was the table, with a red table cloth, 12 magenta roses, dinner (5 course) all set and ready to go, and most importantly, a card.

104

in which he wrote that I have nothing to worry about, especially in Cancun. Then there were heart shaped sugar cookies...it was a perfect evening. We cuddled for like 4 hours, he had all the food ready, and his room was immaculate. He is the perfect guy, and gave me such a special night that I will never forget.

Matt brought it. Either my days with Matt were phenomenal or really bad. The bad days outnumbered the phenomenal ones, however, when he pulled stunts like this, I forgot about all the bad days; I forgot about everything. He had me–completely and entirely had me. I have always been a sucker for romantic gestures such as this–it is naturally my love language. It really gets me every time. It does not matter if it involves roses, food, wine, candy, or anything else; to me, it means that someone else took the time to do something nice for me. And that goes a long way.

March 2, 2001

> Well, I stayed up till 3am playing beer pong, but did well on my tests. Then, I went back over to Matt's. He took me out to lunch and he told me I am so prettier by the day. I cried before he left and he said that he was a little sad too. I really don't wanna worry about Matt when I should be having a fun time. You know you'll regret your emotions if you let this get to you. Everything will be fine.

THIS! Why could I have not written this on repeat? My goodness. Matt and I were about to embark on separate spring breaks and I was sad to be leaving him for a week. For those young adults in relationships–read this entry on repeat. I had a glimpse of strength and reality and wish I could have lived by these words for the remainder of my sophomore year. I strongly suggest you try. *Stop worrying about the things you cannot control and start enjoying YOUR life!*

We returned to campus after separate spring breaks. I was so happy to be back with Matt. Temporarily.

March 15, 2001

I made breakfast for Matt today, and then he basically threw a tantrum when I didn't put his jeans in the dryer — I eventually did but today was when I realized that I am spoiling him so much! Everything is awesome tho. The NCAA b-ball is starting today. So I am going to drink tonight. Matt called just to say hi. We are doing the brackets tomorrow. Jay and I made a CD for Kathy. Tonight it's so fun!

My eyes were opening to what others had been saying—Matt took me for granted and did not appreciate the things I did for him. My roommates and girlfriends started pointing little things out. Then, Psycho Mike, of all people, said I would never break up with him no matter what Matt did. It was weighing heavily on me. Matt got real used to me doing his laundry and neatly folding it, and the second it was out of place, BAM, I got the third degree. Yelling at me about a pair of undried jeans was a little harsh and unnecessary.

April 3, 2001

TUESDAY 3

Tonight was the JRW Ring premiere, our room is already given away for next year, and I went down to Slavin and I saw a commencement bid sale sign. It hit me then. I walked back and Matt had left a nice message on my machine and I started crying. It's coming so fast and I don't want it to end.

Sophomore year was coming to an end faster than I wanted it to. I was sad it was ending. Things were moving. Things were happening. We had one good month left before it was all over. I was not ready for it. I do not think at any point I envisioned Matt and I staying together while he was in Boston working a real job. I wanted to steer clear of long-distance relationships. In that moment, his approaching departure just hit me like a ton of bricks. I was not necessarily ready for it to end; I just knew that it slowly would.

I needed a break.

May 1, 2001

> TUESDAY 1
>
> all day - thoughts of Matt and I have been battling each other out in my mind stay or Break - wonderful ideas for both sides but I just don't know Matt called and invited me for a movie for wed. Heath called and invited me on a thing - I told him it was strictly friendship and he's all good w/ that, at least what I think. I just don't know - I am just gonna wait and see what happens. It seems like more people are for ending it, but I just can't.

All day – thoughts of Matt and I have been battling each other out in my mind – Stay or Break – wonderful ideas for both sides but I just don't know. Matt called and invited me for a movie for Wednesday. Heath called and invited me on a thing – I told him it was strictly friendship and he's all good with that, at least what I think. I just don't know – I am just gonna wait and see what happens. It seems like more people are for ending it, but I just can't.

It was now May, less than a month away from the close of sophomore year. Matt's senior year was coming to an end, and I paired that with our relationship. I reached out to others for their advice. Typically, you already know which way you are leaning in making decisions. Asking others for their opinions just pulls you in different directions that you did not even know existed and adds more confusion to the mix. I was getting tired of the constant battle in my head over whether our relationship would pan out. It did not help that my eyes were starting to wander.

It was a well-known fact that PC grooms hockey players, many of whom go on to play professionally. I grew up going to Chicago Blackhawks games and thought hockey players were the most attractive athletes ever. One night a couple of us girls headed up to the bars and all the hockey players were standing in a corner. Looking hot. One of them instantly caught my eye. So here is a guy named Heath, who told me he had been drafted *by the Chicago Blackhawks* and had an interest in me. He was a senior. We were strictly friends because I was dating Matt. I had not really hung out with the hockey players; it was not the crowd I was familiar with. I was interested in learning more about this crowd, but then soon found out why I should *not* be exploring new territory.

May 4, 2001

DONE. Done with Civ. Done with classes. Done with Matt (in my mind). I have been drinking since 10:30 am and have had so much fun — fire alarms, fires on the quad, and then Kelly and I went to PT. Heath was there, ignored me, I almost cried, he came and saved me, went to Brads, went home and made out with him. Yes, I cheated on Matt, and I have no regrets. I wanna have fun, like he got to. I want to experience college even if it means losing Matt.

Well, there you have it. I had done something I found so repulsive–I cheated on Matt. I was somewhat in awe of my actions. I fought for Matt for two years and then one drunken night I threw it all away to a hockey player, who, I found out the following night, *was engaged*. So that ended as quickly as it started. I was so disappointed in myself for ruining it on someone who was simply using me.

I was just–done. Emotionally, mentally, physically–done. It was a very freeing yet very terrifying feeling all at once. This was the life that I had known for two years, and I was ready to start my next chapter. The only problem was, I needed to share this with Matt.

In the coming weeks, I focused more on my girlfriends and less on Matt. I wanted to spend my time with my roommates and friends before the year ended. If Matt reached out to me, I was there. But otherwise, I started distancing myself from him. I could not bear to tell him prior to his graduation. I was waiting for the perfect time (news flash–there is no perfect time. Get these hard conversations over with as quickly as possible, otherwise they just hang over your head like a big black cloud).

May 12, 2001

12 SATURDAY HAPPY BIRTHDAY!

my bday rocked- I got a necklace from matt, he took me to b-fast & the beach He did make me cry cuz of a petty little fight but I didn't let that ruin my night - which was good - I had fun ☺ (Its nice to know) that I have friends that call me ☺.

My bday rocked. I got a necklace from Matt, he took me to b-fast & the beach. He did make me cry cuz of a petty little fight but I didn't let that ruin my night – which was good. I had fun. It's nice to know that I have friends that call me.

The roller-coaster of emotions I experienced with Matt for close to two years allowed me to push through a stupid fight *on my birthday*. I did not let it ruin my celebrations. I simply could not continue this relationship with Matt. I had not discussed these feelings with him, but knew it was imminent.

May 20, 2001

20 SUNDAY

Well, today Matt graduated. I melted when I saw him in his gown. Mike and I left during the ceremony to go grab some food. We drank too, it was so random. Then we went out to a nice lunch. We were all exhausted so we didn't party tonight "

Well, today Matt graduated. I melted when I saw him in his gown. Mike and I left during the ceremony to go grab some food. We drank too, it was so random. Then we went out to a nice lunch. We were all exhausted so we didn't party tonight.

That was it. Matt graduated. He looked so handsome in his gown. I wanted to hug him and hold onto him forever in that moment. We had a jam-packed week of graduation activities. We were all just... physically and emotionally exhausted. I retreated to my empty room. My friends and roommate had left; it was just me surrounded by empty boxes that needed to be packed. My heart and my mind needed rest. Packing would wait another day.

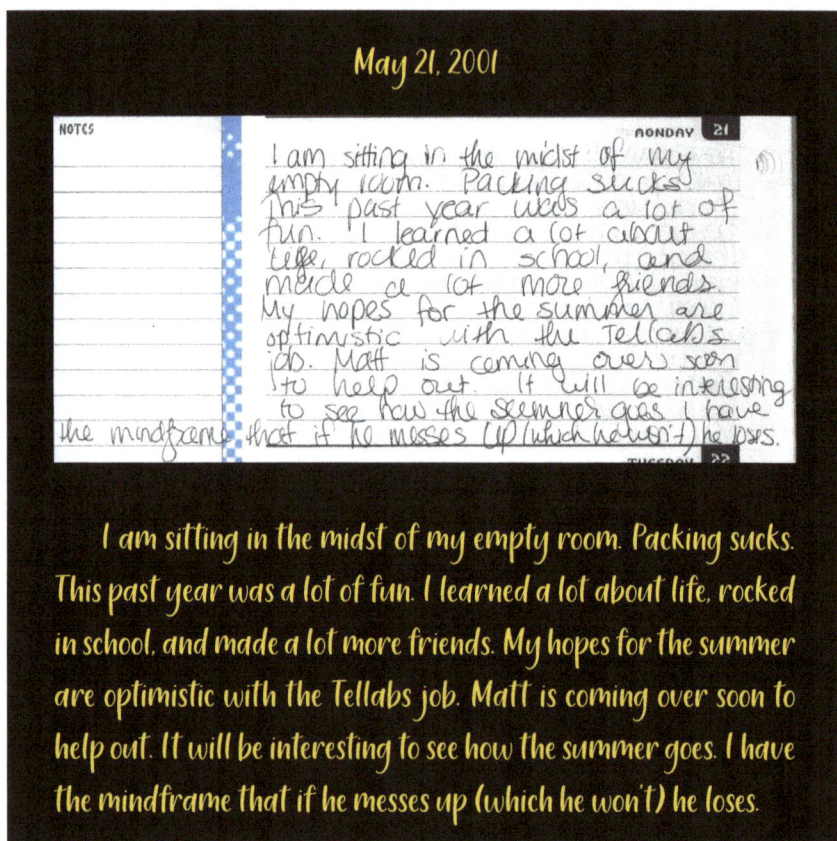

May 21, 2001

I am sitting in the midst of my empty room. Packing sucks. This past year was a lot of fun. I learned a lot about life, rocked in school, and made a lot more friends. My hopes for the summer are optimistic with the Tellabs job. Matt is coming over soon to help out. It will be interesting to see how the summer goes. I have the mindframe that if he messes up (which he won't) he loses.

FINALLY, the desperate girl was gone. My eyes were opened. The ball was in Matt's court to keep the relationship alive. It was sink or swim. After two years of fighting and keeping our relationship going, it was finally *his* turn to push and fight for us. He gave it a valiant effort, but in the end, it was too little, too late.

I officially broke up with Matt on the Fourth of July (because I took Independence Day too literally). The breakup was not easy on either of us—after all, it was two years of our lives and carried a lot of happiness, as well as a lot of sadness. But it was time to move on.

And boy, did I ever.

JUNIOR YEAR

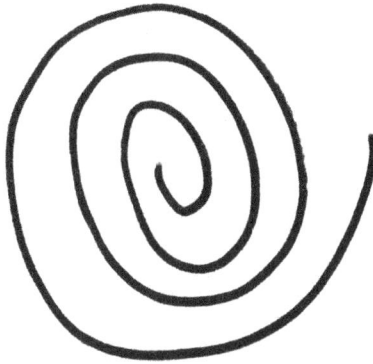

5

UNLEASHED

Junior year. Not my proudest year. There is a vast difference between getting someone's attention and being the center of attention for negative reasons. I quickly went from the first to the latter.

Let me note that when I attended high school, not one guy looked at me. Ever. We had junior and senior year proms. I was not asked to either. I attended senior year prom by default as I went with the only guy remaining in our friends' group. While I sporadically dated in high school, one relationship stood out from the rest. This special boyfriend was a total creep. Creep defined as watching me dial my locker combination and then leaving lingerie in my locker *after* we broke up (I was the ripe young age of fifteen). He also thought it would be fun to find handwritten notes that were intended for but had not been delivered to my girlfriends and share them *with my mother*. These notes detailed all the things that I would never share with my mom, such as who I liked, what party I wished I was invited to, and the other melodramatic things fifteen-year-old girls chat about. Said ex-boyfriend was truly a gem.

Fast-forward to junior year of college. I was in the best shape of my life, a Division I diver, had a strict workout regimen, and was confident with a pretty smile. The boys started looking my way. I craved the attention and never looked back.

In my mind, I was making up for lost time.

Remind you, I had also been dating Matt since starting college. We ended up on different wavelengths, unable to continue dating, and I needed the break. I was beyond ready for this fresh start.

As busy as I was in junior year, it was really an awakening experience. I would not be wrong in saying that some girls need this experience to truly identify who they are–who they want–and who they want to be. Every day was a challenge to determine whether I wanted to date someone or be alone and casually dating. The problem was "casual dating" was just hookups with zero follow-ups. No second dates. I was okay with that–sometimes. Junior year essentially allowed me to be free and be whoever I wanted to be.

I grew a lot junior year.

I moved into an on-campus apartment with Dana, Melissa and Kristen. The two bedrooms were separated by a bathroom/sink/shower combination. Behind the rooms/bathroom was the sitting area with a decent-sized kitchen. We had a small TV/VCR in the corner and a tape/CD player on the opposite side of the sitting area. It was the perfect apartment for the four of us girls and Meg (my Wonderful Roommate) was right down the hallway with her three other roommates.

I was so excited to be back on campus. While I gained a lot of experience while working at a corporate law firm, I was ready to return to school with my friends.

My parents and I had a wonderful early dinner. We hugged and said our goodbyes; they were going to get some rest before driving home. Their plan was to start driving early the next morning and stop halfway through the seventeen-hour drive; rest overnight at a hotel and continue their way back to Chicago–unfortunately for them, that weekend was the New York State Fair and *every single* hotel room was sold out. They continued into Pennsylvania and still could not find any available hotel rooms. Once they made it to Ohio, they started chugging coffee and switching drivers every thirty minutes. They made it back to Chicago, just barely.

August 31, 2001

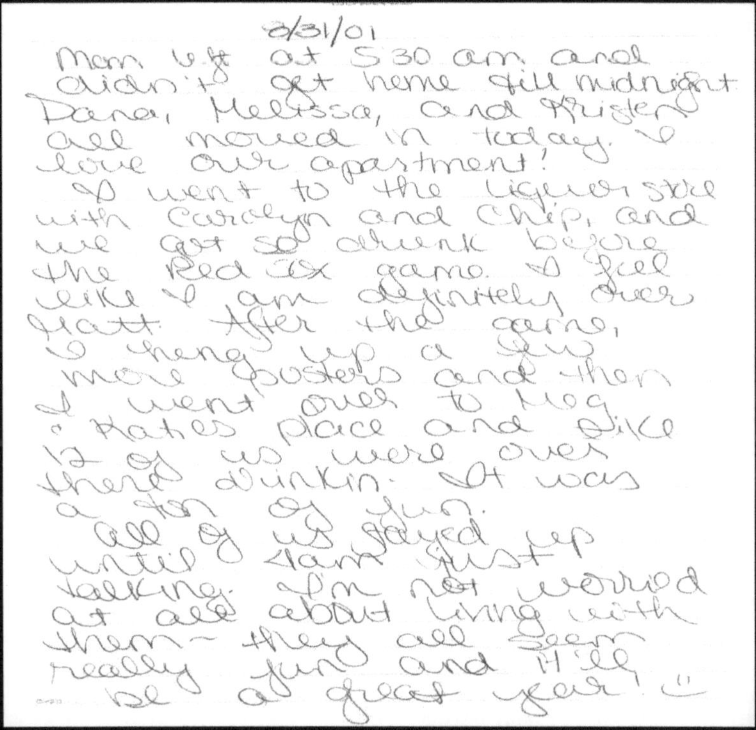
8/31/01
Mom left at 5:30 am and didn't get home till midnight Dana, Melissa, and Kristen all moved in today. I love our apartment! I went to the liquor store with Carolyn and Chip, and we got so drunk before the Red Sox game. I feel like I am definitely over Matt. After the game, I hung up a few more posters and then I went over to Meg & Katies place and like 12 of us were over there drinkin. It was a ton of fun. All of us stayed up until 4am just talking. I'm not worried at all about living with them - they all seem really fun and it'll be a great year! :)

Mom left at 5:30 am and didn't get home till midnight. Dana, Melissa and Kristen all moved in today. I love our apartment! I went to the liquor store with Carolyn and Chip and we got so drunk before the Red Sox game. I feel like I am definitely over Matt. After the game, I hung up a few more posters and then I went over to Meg & Katie's place and like 12 of us were over there drinking. It was a ton of fun. All of us stayed up until 4am just talking. I'm not worried at all about living with them – they all seem really fun and it'll be a great year!

My roommates and girlfriends were the sweetest people I had ever met. There were eight of us in total (my three roommates and Meg's three roommates). We gave Tiffany's necklaces to each other for our twenty-first birthdays, as we celebrated the milestone birthday junior year. (I have since lost mine).

Since college, I always had a close group of girlfriends. I have my inner circle–those girls who I can lean on and have developed very close friendships with, some since grammar school. I know some girls, like my sister, who literally have hundreds of friends. My sister can walk into a room with a ton of people, leave with half of their numbers, and will be Facebook friends with the other half. I am much more of a quiet introvert and only open up after getting to know people better. I have my core group and stick with them; I do not see anything wrong with the contrary. But as a girl in college, I think it is imperative to have your core group of girls. If you do not have your girls, you should rebuild.

There were a handful of times during my junior year I truly just felt like crawling into a deep, dark hole and staying there for a long, long time. Thankfully, these girls kept me out of the dark holes and the thoughts that coincided with those dreadful feelings. Keep your girlfriends close. Those are the best friendships you will ever have. Always put them first. These friendships were the backbone of my college life, and I do not know what I would have done without them!

I had no hesitation returning to the college bars with my girlfriends, but it was–weird–being free. Matt was essentially my security blanket for two years and he was no longer in the picture. Well, he *wanted* to be in the picture. After I broke up with him, he "realized what he had lost" and did everything in his power to fix our relationship. It was just too late. The damage had been done. He really hurt me, especially towards the end, and I was ready for my fresh start and exploring my single life. I was *not* ready for the repercussions.

I wasted no time diving into junior year.

September 1, 2001

Yea, so, tonight, Chip, Carolyn, Lindsey and Ryan and I were all drinking in my apartment. Well then we went to Brad's. But before that, Carolyn and I went to go pick up alcohol and 2 cops watched us jump the fence then we came back with alcohol and talked to them! So tonight after Brad's, Ryan, Lyndsey and I all went to Clubbies. Lyndsey and I had a bet to see who would hook up first—I did! In Clubbies! Worst part—with Mike. —Mike's best friend! He's so hot. But so random. Had fun.

Truly, the best way to really mess with your ex is to hook up with his younger brother's best friend. I remember seeing Mike B. at parties–but of course nothing had happened in those two years. And then BAM, I become single and kiss someone on the Don't Kiss List.

I would suggest staying away from the ex's siblings and/or friends. Once you start including other family members and/or their friends in your breakups, it goes from dirty to wicked rather quickly. It is never a pleasant experience–not even a little bit.

September 7, 2001

> 9/7/01
>
> Today was such a nice day. I began w/ fruit loops for breakfast - they were so good! :" Classes went by fast, and for lunch I had it w/ woody & another hockey player! In the afternoon, Carolyn and I went to the liquor store, and on our way back, I was holding the 12-pack and I walked into the elevator. Brian was in there and said what are you doing tonight? I said This. He said stop by tonight!

Today was such a nice day. I began with fruitloops[1] for breakfast – they were so good. Classes went by fast, and

---

[1] Had I known I documented my meals, I would have reconsidered writing this book.

for lunch I had it with Woody and another hockey player. In the afternoon, Carolyn and I went to the liquor store and on our way back, I was holding the 12-pack and I walked into elevator. Brian was in there and said what are you doing tonight? I said this. He said stop by tonight.

Our on-campus apartment was a co-ed dorm and Brian lived across the hall. We frequently crossed paths while we were moving in and going to and from classes. I would often take note of him–he was always well dressed and incredibly good-looking. Apparently, he took notice of me too.

Brian is not the one who got away. Brian is the one I had to get away *from*. He was of a different breed. An Italian Job. The iconic tall, dark, and handsome with deep blue eyes. New York accent, solid build. Unfortunately, he took interest in me and was exceptionally smooth. I simply could not resist. When he told me he grew up in the Hamptons, I knew he came from money, and he offered to take me on adventures I could have only dreamed about.

September 9, 2001

9/9/01

OH MY GOSH! So this morning at 6am, Brian & I drove to Ct. to get the ferry to Long Island. He's so cute — he told me to fall asleep on the way there & and then he fell asleep on me on the ferry. I met his mom who picked us up. We went to his house and its so cute. Then me, him, his dad, & uncle went thru NYC (its amazing) to New Jersey for the game. It was really hot but really fun. Then Mrs. made us dinner w/ candles — they are so Italian. laughing and talking loud and everything. We almost missed the ferry ride back cuz she got pulled over! But we made it back and he still wanted to hang out with me when we got back so I slept over! I actually slept, too. I love the way that he treats me. He is so nice, and HOT! I feel like I always smile when I am with him. I still don't know if I would want a relationship, just cuz I don't want my freedom taken away....

Oh my gosh! So this morning at 6am, Brian and I drove to Ct. to get the ferry to Long Island. He's so cute — he told me to fall asleep on the way there and then he fell asleep on me on the ferry. I met his mom who picked us up. We went to his house and

> its so cute. Then me, him, his dad, & uncle went thru NYC (it's amazing) to New Jersey for the game. It was really hot but really fun. Then Mrs. D made us dinner w/ candles — they are so Italian laughing and talking loud and everything. We almost missed the ferry ride back cuz she got pulled over! But we made it back and he still wanted to hang out with me when we got back so I slept over! I actually slept, too. I love the way that he treats me. He is so nice and HOT! I feel like I always smile when I am with him. I still don't know if I would want a relationship, just cuz I don't want my freedom taken away.

Brian is credited with taking me to New York two days before 9/11. It was a bright, sunny day and we were driving through the city enroute to the New York Jets game. We passed under a viaduct and when I looked up, I saw the stunning Twin Towers glistening in the sun. I was in awe. It was a beautiful sight—an image that will stay with me forever. As much as I regret my relationship with Brian, I briefly saw those magnificent towers. While I grew up in Chicago, seeing the New York skyline was different. The buildings were taller, bigger, and the skyline was longer; expanding over many more miles.

A mere forty-eight hours later, terrorists flew a plane into each of those brilliant towers, ultimately bringing them down, along with too much death and destruction to comprehend. Thousands of innocent people were killed in those towers and the immediate vicinity. My room-mate Dana and I were getting ready for class and instead of watching the Price is Right, which we did every morning, our eyes were met with these towers that I had just seen two days prior, now with a glaring hole in the side and flames bursting through. Just while we were attempting to comprehend what we were seeing, a second plane hit the second tower and erupted into flames. At first, there were reports that a private jet had flown into the tower. But after the second plane was flown into the tower, we knew this was no accident. And then news broke that another plane flew into the Pentagon, killing hundreds more, and a fourth plane was taken down in Pennsylvania, killing all on board.

Our sacred country was under attack. I fell to my knees as the first tower collapsed. We were crying and stared at the TV in complete horror as the second tower fell. Dana and I felt sick to our stomachs and completely useless. What was happening? *How* could this be happening? Hours later, there were news reports that a terrorist was arrested a few blocks from our school. It turned out to be false, but we were terrified.

Of the four thousand people at my school, it was reported a quarter of them lost a family member on 9/11. One of the flight attendants lived in the apartments down the street from campus. My teammate's brother was in the north tower above where the plane hit. He was told to go to the roof of the building; helicopters were going to save him. He was calm and ready to be rescued. We were later told it was way too hot and smokey for the helicopters to attempt rescue missions.

Our campus was somber for months after 9/11. Everyone was a little quieter. The world was forever changed on September 11, 2001, as terrorists destroyed that amazing skyline and so many families. It was a frightening and unsure time, but I am thankful I had a glimpse of the city, which will stay with me forever.

While our hearts remained heavy, college moved forward.

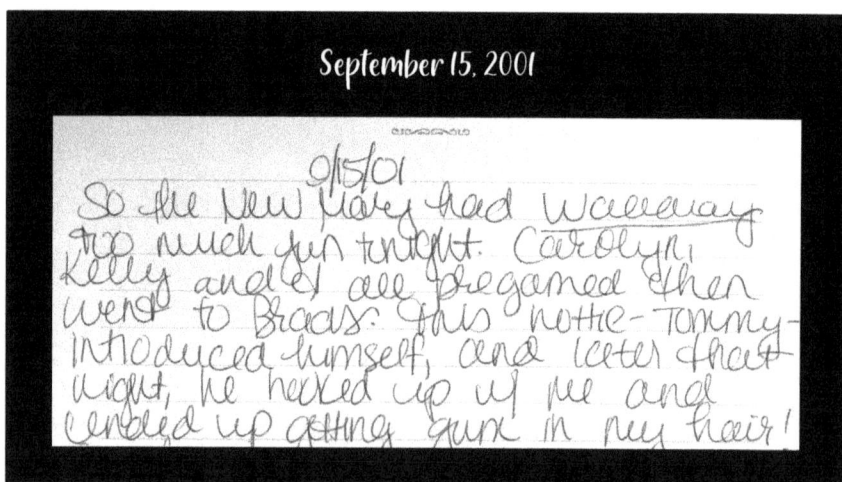

September 15, 2001

So the New Mary had waaaaay too much fun tonight. Carolyn, Kelly and I all pregamed then went to Brad's. This hottie – Tommy – introduced himself, and later that night he hooked up with me and ended up getting gum in my hair!

Carolyn, Kelly, and I picked up where we left off and frequently visited our favorite bar, Brad's. It was the upperclassmen bar. Brad's was within walking distance to campus, had great drink specials, and a hot bartender. Carolyn, Kelly, and I sat at the bar and quickly started getting free shots from Tommy the bartender. We were not mad about it and he was enjoying the entertainment. The free drinks and shots kept coming, as well as the witty one-liners that he must have used on hundreds of girls, but I fell for them. During one of his breaks, he told me to follow him. Carolyn and Kelly gave me a wink as I hopped off the high bar stool and Tommy led the way. He walked me to the side of the bar that was out of plain sight and into a dark, narrow closet, barely big enough for two people standing. I started giggling and he grabbed me around my waist and started kissing me. We were in that closet for a fun couple of minutes before composing ourselves and heading back to the bar. Before I could even sit down, Carolyn blurted out *"What is in your hair?"* I grabbed my long hair into my left hand, and it was met with–gum. Tommy's gum somehow ended up in my hair. Thankfully, it was towards the bottom, so we laughed as we cut it free from my hair. I learned through Tommy that hanging with a bartender, getting free drinks, and making out in a dark closet was fun, but getting gum stuck in my hair was not.

September 16, 2001

9/16/01

Today was Really just a day of looking over this crazy weekend. I felt justified after talking to Beth cuz she says I am just testing my freedom. Monica said- everyone hooks up! Brian has to be my favorite cuz a) hes taking things reeeal slow b) hot new date c) calls like everyday d) friends seem to like me. But for some reason, I am just attracted to the wild side of the hockey players although the risk of being quickly dumped is at about 95% Just the fun of hooking up w/ one is over. But in the long term, the Road to Brian looks the brightest. Nick sent me such a nice email. Melissa's mom made awesome lasagna- everything else is going well!

Today was really just a day of looking over this crazy weekend. I felt justified after talking to Beth cuz she says I am just testing my freedom. Monica said — everyone hooks up! Brian has to be my favorite cuz a) he's taking things reeeal slow

b) hot JRW date c) calls like everyday d) friends seem to like me. But for some reason, I am just attracted to the wild side of the hockey players although the risk of being quickly dumped is at about 95%. Just the fun of hooking up w/ one is cool. But in the long term, the road to Brian looks the brightest. Nick sent me such a nice email. Melissa's mom made awesome lasagna — everything else is going well!

The juggling act had begun, and I did not know how to juggle. Nick was still in the picture. We hung out the entire summer before I returned junior year. Each summer, we grew immensely closer. We just never committed ourselves to each other as we were a thousand miles apart. I did not want to worry about what he was doing nor did I want to be tied down with anyone, even though I very much cared for Nick.

Although I enjoyed hanging out with Brian, he grew tired of me not knowing whether I wanted to settle down with him. I did and I didn't. It literally changed by the hour. And at the eleventh hour, I decided I needed to further explore my new single life.

And that I did.

September 22, 2001

9/22/01

Nick called me today and he gave me this fun personality quiz. I was laughing really hard cuz it was funny, and when I got off the phone, Kristen said I never heard you laugh as much as you do with Nick!

Nick called me today and he gave me this personality quiz. I was laughing really hard cuz it was funny, and when I got off the phone, Kristen said I never heard you laugh as much as you do with Nick!

My roommate, Kristen, was right. Even though Nick was a thousand miles away, we always just *clicked*. We laughed together. We spent hours on the phone without it feeling like hours at all. We were just too far away to make it work.

October 1, 2001

> Michelle Branch's song could best describe me now – "So lonely inside, so busy out there, and all you wanted was somebody who cares."

Are there songs in your life that take you back to a moment in time? If you play any Michelle Branch song, it brings me back to junior year. Her lyrics were spot on for everything I was experiencing. I *was* so busy out there–exploring all my options. But at the end of the day, when I retreated to my room by myself, I was so lonely. I needed to mentally and emotionally hit the Reset button, so I headed home for Columbus Day Weekend.

October 6, 2001

10/6/01

Mom and I went shopping all day today. I would say I'm excited to eat but we had a huge breakfast. This sounds bad, but I'm really not too excited to see Nick. I mean, what we had was a total summer fling. I went off and experienced this whole new life, and I come back, and although it shouldn't matter about his stoopid oreccas, they are still a turn-off.

Matt called this morning too. He has a like whole day set up for him- me in Boston. I think I might decline that offer.

I feel like a completely different person. Matt ruled my life for 2 years, now I can't stand him. Nick, probably the one person who will ever treat me like a Princess, I'm no longer attracted to. This is a huge identity problem, and I have really never felt this alone before.

Mom and I went shopping all day today. I would say I'm excited to eat but we had a huge breakfast. This sounds bad but I'm really not too excited to see Nick. I mean, what we had was a total summer fling. I went off and experienced this whole new life, and I come back, and although it shouldn't matter about his stupid dreads, they are still a turn-off. Matt called this morning too. He has a like whole day set up for him & me in Boston. I think I might decline that offer. I feel like a completely different person. Matt ruled my life for 2 years, now I can't stand him. Nick, probably the one person who will ever treat me like a princess, I'm no longer attracted to. This is a huge identity problem, and I have really never felt this alone before.

Returning for Columbus Day weekend threw a wrench into my life. I was so confused; I enjoyed being home and hanging out with Nick, but I could not enjoy myself too much as I would return to the East Coast days later and would suffer a lot of heartache.

Matt was still trying to be in the picture. He was rolling out the red carpet for me and trying to get back together. I wanted nothing to do with him. Although the attention he gave to me was appreciated, it was still too late.

All in all, it was just a tumultuous time in my life. And sometimes the chaos is okay. Sometimes you need to be at the bottom to sort everything out before you can get to the top. But that is exactly where I was, the bottom.

October 10, 2001

10/10/01

OAR. Sarah and I drove up to Boston college and met up with her hottie freshmen cousin. We forgot the tix in Sarahs car which was parked so far away, but it was amusing. So we all (or maybe just me) got wasted before hand (while waiting for the bus we peed in the bushes. The concert itself was ok, fun, but not impressive. I had a quote "I am beyond intoxicated" I was falling all over the T on our way there, and I smoked like a chimney! Sarah and I took some awesome pics. We never met up w/ Jay but I didn't feel like seeing him anyways. We ordered late night chinese and I passed out. I woke up (5 hrs later) still drunk, we crawled across BC (and got eyed at :) and came back fun night!!

OAR. Sarah and I drove up to Boston College and met up with her hottie freshman cousin. We forgot the tix in Sarah's car which was parked so far away, but it was amusing. So we all (or maybe just me) got wasted before hand (while waiting for the bus we peed in the bushes). The concert itself was ok, fun, but not impressive. I had a quote "I am beyond intoxicated." I was falling all over the T on our way there, and I smoked like a chimney! Sarah and I took some awesome pics. We never met up w/ Jay but I didn't feel like seein him anyways. We ordered late night Chinese and I passed out. I woke up (5 hours later) still drunk. We crawled across BC (and got eyed at) and came back. Fun night!

As mentioned, Sarah and I established a really strong friendship with Ryan and Jay sophomore year, and almost every time we were in their room, O.A.R. would be blasting through the speakers. O.A.R. (Of a Revolution)–is an incredibly talented band from the East Coast with catchy songs. They played at a ton of college bars starting in 1996. Anytime they were anywhere near PC, we attended. This night was like every other concert, except I had a little too much to drink and could not even appreciate their amazing show.

It is one thing to drink at a concert; it is another to get completely inebriated to a point where you cannot even appreciate the music. I suggest taking it easy and enjoying the show. You will appreciate the music just a little bit more.

October 14, 2001

> 10/14/01
> Well last night I wrote an email to Nick sayin that I don't think it'd work for us anymore and he responded saying that I was wrong. I just don't want to be in a relationship w/ him and I wish that he could understand.

Well last night I wrote an email to Nick sayin that I didn't think it'd work for us anymore and he responded saying that I was wrong. I just don't want to be in a relationship w/ him and I wish that he could understand.

Although I cared for Nick, I thought it simply was not fair to him that I was exploring East Coast territory. I tried breaking things off for his protection, but he stayed in the picture for much longer, unfortunately for him. While we seamlessly connected with each other over college breaks, continuing this "friendship" was simply a recipe for disaster.

October 16, 2001

Classes went by fast, then at diving, I did the trampoline w/ music going (Michelle Branch). Newell came in and we did clown dives~ it just put me in this mood like I can do anything. Lotsa fun. Then Lee, me, Lyndsay, and Anne (my swim family) took us to Caf Paragon~ so good~ and then to Ben & Jerrys!

Classes went by fast, then at diving, I did the trampoline w/ music going (Michelle Branch). Newell came in and we did clown dives – it just put me in this mood like I can do anything. Lotsa fun. Then Lee, me, Lyndsay, and Anne (my swim family) took us to Café Paragon – so good – and then to Ben & Jerry's!

Clown dives are dives that are done in front of a crowd to garner laughter. Diving that day was simply a burn day; nothing was accomplished.

When I started freshman year, I was joined by five freshman teammates. Year by year, another teammate would quit until junior year, where I was the only remaining diver from our core group. Our coach, Newell, had two young children and was not there as a full-time coach. I ended up stepping into the role for the new divers to at least give them *some* guidance. I often wanted to quit myself. It was hard navigating on my own and staying motivated, but that seemed to be the theme junior year, so I stuck with it.

October 25, 2001

> Tonight, Ryan & Liam cooked Kristen and I dinner – it was real good – we had steak... it was amusing when I was using the wrong side of the steak knife to cut my steak! Liam & I were very cuddly. His personality is so great and he's so nice, but he is just not my type – and it's hard to look beyond that. I definitely still don't wanna have a boyfriend – I just wanna settle down – if that makes sense...

My roommate, Kristen, had been dating Ryan for quite some time and she thought Ryan's roommate–Liam–and I should be introduced. They had us over for dinner and it was wonderful. Liam was such a gentleman, however, I learned I was not ready to settle down with the nice guy. I was still in the asshole phase and apparently liked getting gum stuck in my hair and going after the "hot" guys that I had no business associating myself with. It literally took me a decade to figure out that attractive *and* nice guys do exist; I was lucky enough to marry one! But in the meantime, I was too busy chasing the assholes.

October 31, 2001

So tonight, we all dressed up as army chicks! We went to Primetime and it was pretty fun! I drank a ton—and we stopped at Golden Crust. I kissed & flirted w/ a hottie Brooke who is so cute! Night!

Halloween was always a memorable night. The eight of us girls dressed up and loved seeing our other friends dressed up too. The even better party was at the late-night food stop to fill our stomachs with grease before retreating to our room. How I remained fit during college is still a mystery to me, but if you learn and practice *moderation,* you will be okay. I did not, however, practice moderation and solely wanted to practice kissing. I certainly could not help myself after running into a current classmate of mine who was irresistibly cute.

November 2, 2001

11/2/01

In general- a bad day. I got a 75 on my "easy" history midterm, which completely upset me for the rest of the day. Then I went to diving and it didn't get any better- 3 meter kicked the shit outta me. I smacked a lot and ended up crying cuz I was so frustrated.

I think I am just wishing that I was at home cuz it was just pure fun and I need to get away from all this work and stress. I have too many things that I am looking forward to at home.

Tonight, the senior girls cooked us pasta. It was real good. I can't believe next year it'll be us "! Then Kate, Kelly and I went to the hockey game. Kate & I talked about sex and I feel less guilty - its college, and I am young & single.

In general — a bad day. I got a 75 on my "easy" history midterm, which completely upset me for the rest of the day. Then I went to diving and it didn't get any better — 3 meter

> kicked the shit outta me. I smacked a lot and ended up crying cuz I was so frustrated. I think I am just wishing I was at home cuz it was just pure fun and I need to get away from this work and stress. I have too many things that I am looking forward to at home. Tonight, the senior girls cooked us pasta. It was real good. I can't believe next year it'll be us. Then Kate, Kelly and I went to the hockey game. Kate and I talked about sex and I feel less guilty – its college, and I am young and single.

You know those days that you just feel–gross? Like you do not want to get up and face the world; you just want to bury yourself under a blanket and call it a day? That was junior year. Not a day, the year. It was tough because I was discovering myself (and that was scary). I was growing up. I started having responsibilities. I was not easily coasting along in school anymore after being so well-prepared, and it was catching up. Smacking off three meter (a ten foot fall into the water) sure did not help. It was like the water was punishing me. Or smacking some sense into me–not sure which. I was far from being able to qualify for the BIG EAST and felt so defeated and lost. I did not know what I wanted.

Frankly, I did not know who I was, either. Some days I wanted to get dressed up and be the pretty girl, and most other days I just wanted to hide. It is amazing how quickly you can go from being on top of the world to being in such a lost little place.

Thankfully, Class Act Kate remained a very close friend. We were always on the same wavelength. We lived a floor apart freshman year, down the hall sophomore year, and remained teammates through senior year. We were both history majors and understood the importance of balancing school and athletics. We always had a complete blast hanging out and grew into a dangerous duo our junior year as we had both ended long-term relationships. She validated my actions. We were able to confide in each other. I was grateful for my strong friendship with Class Act Kate.

November 3, 2001

Today was our first meet. I was real nervous and so I fucked up on 1 meter, but I came 14 pts from winning 3m. The girls won the meet and the guys lost. It was kinda weird w/out Matt there, but enjoyable cuz I could talk to other people. And Jamie won the meet which is awesome.

November 16, 2001

11/16/01

Matt called today saying that he didn't want to talk anymore cuz I haven't called him so I replied very well and he felt stupid & apologized. It's exactly what I don't miss about him – his stupid – not thought through ideas. I feel like I have no heart anymore and all I have been doing is breaking other hearts.

This was Matt's final attempt at keeping an open line of communication between us. It did not go well for him. I was done with Matt and over his games. I was thankful for his surrender but could not help feeling sad about hurting him.

November 17, 2001

> 11/17/01
>
> We had our diving meet today. I sucked on 1 meter but rocked on 3. Jamie beat me by 8 points! At night, I went to Brad's where I met Shamois, and he took me to Old's, then we hooked up... I hardly knew him...

We had our diving meet today. I sucked on 1 meter but rocked on 3. Jamie beat me by 8 points. At night, I went to Brad's where I met Shamois and he took me to Old's, then we hooked up... I hardly know him...

November 26, 2001

> Today at practice, I found out that Shamois purposely took me to Evans bed because the night before, he had had some girl in it who peed all over his bed! So I slept in dry pee. GROSS

Today at practice, I found out that Shamois purposely took me to Evan's bed because the night before, he had some girl in it who peed all over his bed! So I slept in dry pee. GROSS.

I was continuing on my Kissing Crusade. Apparently, I had graduated from gum in my hair to making out with someone who knew, but failed to inform me, that he did not wash the sheets from the night before. Apparently, the girl he took home the night prior *peed* in his bed and it was not cleaned up. I was quite disgusted by this and myself in general. A note to college attendees in general–please wash your sheets. Regularly.

Although I was exploring my freedom, it was not quite as fun as I thought it would be. It was wonderful being independent and steering my own ship, but I was navigating the waters without a compass. I knew I needed to change course–I was just not sure how.

December 15, 2001

This should be noted – 2 guys at Primetime wanted to dance with me and I said no! Then Herman called twice so I called him back and he asked me over and I also said no! Yay for me.

I was halfway through junior year. After a busy and wild start, I began pulling back the reins. I was at the point where I did not even want the attention anymore; I wanted the opposite of it. I said no to everything. I was closing myself off to the world–that was the only way I knew how to protect myself. I stayed in–a lot, and when I decided to hang out with friends, I was cautious about the amount I was drinking and who I was drinking with. I was still at the bottom and felt like there was no ladder to climb up.

To make matters worse, Herman, the European assistant swim coach, was reaching out to me. He had an accent, blond hair, blue eyes, and dimples. Bells, alarms, and whistles were all sounding in my head–NO! A note to any collegiate athlete, or any college student in general: do not sleep with the swim coach–or any coach. It does not enhance one's reputation. In fact, while it may seem like the most intriguing and enticing action, it is not. It is simply not worth it. Ever. The instant regret and the whispers behind your back solidify it. I would guess at that time, maybe one would be excited to be receiving attention from the assistant swim coach, but alas, what mid-twenties ripped swim coach *would not* have their eyes on college girls? Professional ones, I presume. Please make good decisions and if not, prepare yourself for the repercussions.

I welcomed Winter Break and excitedly spent time at home. We sadly did not attend a winter training trip, but I was able to catch up on sleep, celebrated Christmas with my family, and vowed to start over when I returned to campus. I also worked at the law firm to make some extra cash over the holidays.

December 26, 2001

12/26/01
Today was incredible! I was listening to the radio, and I WON Barenaked Ladies tickets! Hooray! Kathy's going to go with me! Then Nick and I went out to dinner. Its a real shame that we don't have what we did over the summer. He got me a CD for Christmas! ☺.

> Today was incredible! I was listening to the radio and I WON Barenaked Ladies tickets! Hooray! Kathy is going to go with me! Then Nick and I went out to dinner. It's a real shame that we don't have what we did over the summer. He got me a CD for Christmas!

My heart skipped a beat when the radio DJ said "be caller ten." I quickly dialed the number and held my breath as the line started ringing and the DJ answered with as much excitement as was sitting on my chest. "Congratulations, you're the tenth caller. What is your name?"

I had to quickly find my voice and exclaim "Mary!" After he collected my information, I immediately called my sister. We attended the Barenaked Ladies New Years Eve concert and our seats were within spitting distance to the stage. It took everything I had to keep it together and not explode with excitement! The concert was thrilling! Balloons and confetti dropped from the ceiling at midnight. I watched my favorite musicians do a champagne toast and then continue playing my favorite songs. I never wanted that show to end, but certainly had the best time with my sister!

On the other hand, it was a seesaw of emotions with Nick. One night we had the best time ever; the next night I wanted nothing to do with him and questioned why I was even hanging out with him. Maybe I was just trying to protect myself as I knew I would not see him again until the summer. I enjoyed my freedom too much, but I also could not look past the man who was right in front of me who offered everything I had ever wanted.

January 9, 2002

> 1/9/02- Well, today at work, Susan offered the
> summer job to me. But I don't know
> what's gonna happen- the circus or
> tellabs. we shall see- I really wanna
> do the circus tho I think it'll be
> fun! Nick and I went rollerblading
> tonight. It was great weather!

Well, today at work, Susan offered the summer job to me.
But I don't know what's going to happen – the circus or Tellabs.
We shall see – I really wanna do the circus tho I think it'll be fun!
Nick and I went rollerblading tonight. It was great weather!

In January, I was presented with a tough decision of how I would spend my upcoming summer break–returning to the law firm or joining the circus (a term coined by my parents).

"The circus" (also known as the All-American High Dive Team) was a group of kids who traveled across the country putting on twenty-minute shows five times a day at various state fairs. The show had a kid-friendly plot, which consisted of pirates trying to get the treasure from the mermaid all while jumping off thirty-, fifty-, sixty- and eighty-foot platforms into ten feet of water.

When I had just started diving at around age sixteen, I had stumbled upon the circus when they performed at the Taste of Chicago. They were diving off eighty-foot platforms and I was in complete awe. After the show ended, I approached the diving tank and spoke with one of the divers, Carl Kupper, who was also the head diving coach for the North Carolina Tar Heels (rest in peace, my dear friend). I asked Carl what I had to do to be a part of the show. He rattled off the standard requirements, including the fact I had to be twenty-one. I was immediately hooked. Challenge accepted. I followed his instructions, worked on my dives, and updated him about my continued interest thereafter.

The circus sounded *way* more appealing than working in an office.

But I had a lot of decisions to make, and they were weighing heavily on my mind. It was really the first time in my life I had decisions to make, and was allowed to make, for myself. I was in the driver's seat, and it was scary as hell. I emailed one of the attorneys I worked with at the law firm–and wish I saw his face after reading my call for help! The email simply read "Should I dive all summer or work in an office?!" He sent me a half-kidding, half-scathing email response telling me there is no decision to be made. Go dive! Looking back, the situation was laughable. Although you will be presented with tough decisions throughout your life (or what you perceive as being tough), you must weigh everything in front of you, make your selection, and then own it. I have learned the hard way and have teeter-tottered so many times, but the choices I have made with confidence have been the best ones yet. Own it and roll with it. And whatever you do, *do not let outside influences determine your decision*. It is *your* decision after all.

January 19, 2002

> the DIVING MEET! Hooray for me! I'm on the internet got it! yay! So I definetly celebrated my ass off for it too Brian and I drank and watched the Bears lose'. But then I went to the swim team alumni party, Carolyn and I broke the table and on the way out, I fell on my ass cuz of the snow! I' was so drunk' We headed over to the Abbey, where I did THREE carbombs Joey 'and I walked back and I puked allll over. It was horrible.

I WON THE DIVING MEET! Hooray for me! I'm on the internet for it! Yay! So I definitely celebrated my ass off for it too. Brian and I drank and watched the Bears lose. But then I went to the swim team alumni party, Carolyn and I broke the table and on the way out, I fell on my ass cuz of the snow! I was so drunk! We headed over to the Abbey, where I did THREE carbombs. Joey and I walked back and I puked all over. It was horrible.

To note, I *always* placed second at diving meets. I was the queen of coming in second place, never first. I do not know if it was a mental block or what. I could write an entire book on the Mentality Needed to Compete in Collegiate Sports. There is absolutely a science behind it–it is all mental. Well, 80 percent mental and 20 percent body mechanics. You know how to do the sport, but then you add the pressure, the nerves, the crowd; some people embrace that (which I needed to do) and others fold under pressure (which I did). And then the meet is over, and I am left asking, what just happened? I know how to rock these dives, but I would crumble.

BUT the point was that I *finally* WON. And I was thrilled! I was on a high! The internet was still an up-and-coming technological advancement, and PC would release "Sports Highlights" from the weekend. Second place finishers were never mentioned. First place finishers were headlined! Celebrations were in order! And celebrations were had–all day. Drinking and watching football with Brian followed by drinking with my best friend, Carolyn. And then drinking with my best friends' brother, Joey, who was on campus for alumni weekend. The same Joey who was also Matt's very good friend and prior roommate. Joey had the most gorgeous blue eyes on the planet. He was the smartest man I had ever met (besides for my dad, of course). Carolyn, Joey, and I did three car bombs to conclude the Celebratory Day of Drinking. Bars closed and we were in the midst of a blizzard; if Joey did not walk Carolyn and I back to campus, it would have been bad. It still was bad…

I was *so excited* to be hanging out with Joey. We dropped Carolyn off at her dorm and then retreated to my apartment. We were having too much fun and did not want our night to end. Here was my chance! I had waited three years for this moment! We sat on my bed and started talking about the day and how much fun we had. Then he leaned in for a kiss and I met him for the kiss. He gently leaned me back, so I was laying on my bed. It was so wonderful. We were moving right…along…oh my goodness…NO. NO! I sat up quickly, barely in time to projectile vomit all over my bed. The wall. The floor. My desk. Joey. Humiliated is an understatement. I wanted to crawl under my blanket and disappear. But I could not do that because my blanket and everything around us was covered in brown car bomb, viciously stenched vomit. Joey left. My roommate entered the room and was screaming in disgust about the smell. I was wasted and had to clean up my mess, but I was a mess too. How badly I wanted to find that deep dark hole, crawl into it, and never come out.

Instead, I somehow doused my room in Clorox, gathered my bedding, and went to the basement of our apartment to do laundry while the entire night replayed in my head. I sat on the cold basement floor hitting my head against the washing machine in disgust, chugging water, and sitting in my own self-pity, waiting for everything to dry. I climbed into bed while my roommate was sneering at me and vowed to start taking responsibility for my actions. I could not continue this Kissing Crusade any longer; each time became more and more of a disaster. Thankfully, things started looking up.

January 29, 2002

> Probably one of the coolest days! First, I got a call from the circus telling me that I need to fill out an application. Yay! Then, it was like 60-65° out here — so beautiful — and we had class outside! It was real cool. Then, Kristen and I went to the Billy Joel/Elton John concert. Most amazing concert ever. They opened with Your Song — the huge pianos were across from each other — just an unreal show that kept me in awe the whole time. Definitely pure fun!

What is not in this entry is that my friends, Kate and Monica "joined" us at the concert as well. We were poor college students who were lucky to be at the show; we had just enough money to get tickets in the last row in the last section at the highest level. We were happy to be in the same arena as these megastars and did not care what our seating arrangements were. Kate and Monica volunteered to grab the first round of beers. They never came back. This is before we had cell phones. We found out later while they were in the concessions line, Billy Joel's lighting guy approached them and gave them *front row* tickets. Their elbows were on the damn stage the entire show! I died when we finally met them at the car after the concert and they told us what happened. But it was still an amazing show! And the circus had called! It was an uplifting and amazing night that I needed so badly. Find those outlets and engage in them as much as you can. I barely afforded that ticket, but it was such an unbelievable night. Sometimes you have to stretch a little and indulge in activities that excite you. Embrace those moments and experiences; they will stay with you forever.

Suddenly, I found myself three-quarters of the way through junior year. Things were looking up, although I was buried in schoolwork and diving, and not to mention, the LSAT—*the* test which determines your readiness for law school.

February 16, 2002

Did not qualify. But both good & bad things came out of it. Nick called & emailed me and New York looked so different, but still beautiful. Tonight, Carolyn and I got wasted, watched movies & ate spikes. It was definitely a fun nite and better than going to PT!

My last diving meet of junior year had concluded, and I did not qualify for the BIG EAST. To say I was disappointed would be an understatement, but I was throwing a pity party for myself and thankfully Carolyn accepted the invitation.

Nothing was going right junior year.

March 26, 2002

3-26-02 - OMG! Meg had a party at her apartment, and there were like 12 of us girls. We all got completely blasted, and then at 10:30, a stripper came! It was insane. he totally got naked which I don't think they're supposed to do! But there was plenty of whip cream, beer, and pictures! so the fun stopped there tho because @ Brads (the stripper came up!)

OMG! Meg had a party at her apartment, and there were like 12 of us girls. We all got completely blasted, and then at 10:30, a stripper came! It was insane. He totally got naked which I don't think they're supposed to do! But there was plenty of whip cream, beer and pictures! So the fun stopped there tho because @ Brad's, the stripper came with!

Meg's birthday was one of the first of our group's twenty-first birthday celebrations. We were all very eager for this exciting milestone. Each of us had our own themes and all ensured each birthday girl had the best possible celebration. Before each party started, we would all chip in and present the birthday girl with her very own Tiffany's necklace. It was a simple heart dangling from a silver chain and it was stunning!

I am not sure where they hired this stripper from, nor had I ever been at a party with one, but I do remember that he was very excited. I was also concerned about the amount of whipped cream—and other liquids—getting on Meg's apartment couches. I do not think the stripper was *supposed* to join us at the bar afterwards, but he invited himself to join the party and was a bit territorial when other guys were talking to us, so we quickly had him excused from the bar and continued to celebrate Meg.

April 9, 2002

OAR concert! Yay! But before that, Ryan drove me to the Kaplan center to get my LSAT midterm. I raised my score by 5 points, which is good, but my score still blows. Then I made caramona burgers for Carolyn & I then took off for the show. We pregamed at Jay's and it was so much fun. I managed to push my way up to second row at the show. They were so much better this time than in Boston, and at the end of the nite, I managed to get a guitar pick!

As much fun as I was having with my friends and attending shows, the next step of my academic career was starting and it freaked me out. I remember being excited but also having no clue what was happening. I was going through the motions but did not grasp the enormity of it. I started working on the next chapter while still in college. Juggling everyday life while also dipping my toes into the future was hard and scary *as hell*. Although I did not become a lawyer, I wish that I had not started law school a short six months after graduation–I had time. It would have been nice to work at a firm for a year or so. But then again, it was not until I was in law school that I discovered I hated it and reached my own conclusion that it was simply not for me.

To all the twenty-year-olds out there, while it is of course much easier said than done–take your time. You do not have to plan your entire life at age twenty; **it is okay not to know**. Make goals for yourself–in this case, maybe at age twenty-five I would have liked to start my career. But I felt like it was such a rush. It is not. Join the circus. Live your life. Travel. Find out what excites you and research different ways you can make a living from those options. If there are people pressuring you, tune them out. They will need to take the back seat and let you run your course. I just wish someone had told me in college, especially at this point–to just **be**. Just enjoy the moment. Of course, I felt it was imperative to have goals and follow through with them at an alarming pace. But there is also nothing wrong with staying focused and *enjoying the moment*. Stop rushing! If anything, your early twenties *is* the best time, in my opinion, to take it slow and really figure out what is best for you. It might not be what others would have chosen for you based on their life experiences, but it is not *their life*. Remember what you want and stick with it.

April 11, 2002

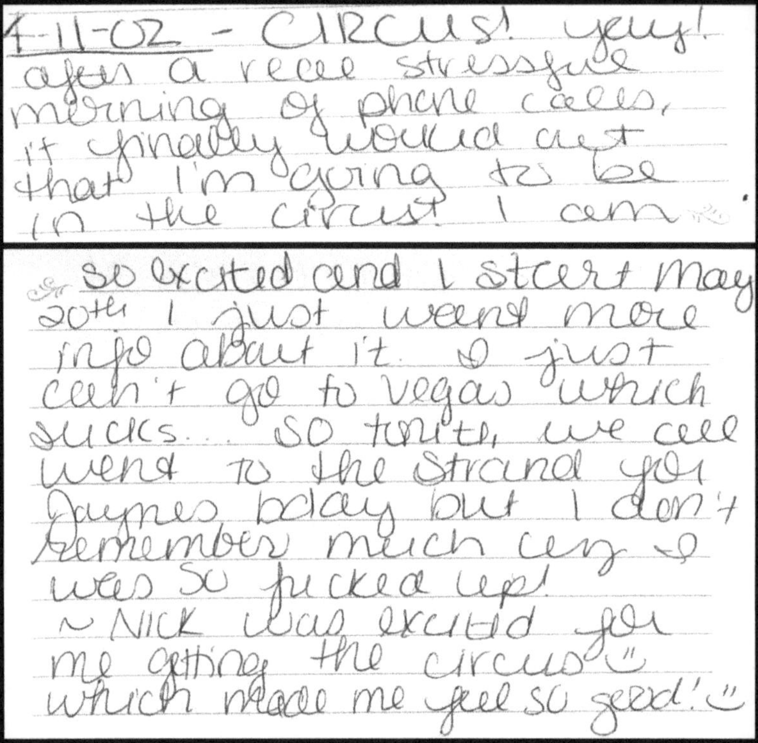
4-11-02 - CIRCUS! yay!
after a real stressful
morning of phone calls,
it finally worked out
that I'm going to be
in the circus! I am
so excited and I start May
20th I just want more
info about it. I just
can't go to Vegas which
sucks... So tonite, we all
went to the Strand for
Jaynes bday but I don't
remember much cuz I
was so fucked up!
~ Nick was excited for
me getting the circus :)
which made me feel so good! :)

Circus! Yay! After a real stressful morning of phone calls, it finally worked out that I'm going to be in the circus! I am so excited and I start May 20th. I just want more info about it. I just can't go to Vegas which sucks. So tonite, we all went to the Strand for Jayne's bday but I don't remember much cuz I was so fucked up. Nick was excited for me getting the circus which made me feel so good!

It was official. I was heading to circus life. My mom planned a twenty-first birthday celebration in Las Vegas with my family the same weekend shows were starting. I called my mom and shared the exciting news about the circus. I was also sad that my entire family would not go to Vegas for my twenty-first birthday as she had planned. Her response (in a friendly but unapologetic voice) "We? No, YOU, cannot go to Vegas. WE are still going."

I got so many phone calls from my family members with screams of "happy birthday!" followed by the sound of coins hitting metal plates after someone hit on slots. I smiled and thanked them, knowing soon enough I would be having my own fun.

May 11, 2002

So I got all dolled up, and my friends came over and then we went to Paragon! I got wine there + I was a little drunk :)

We went back to my room + the pu-game started. Rybo gave me orange rum so I was drinking out of that all nite. It was really awesome having all my friends at my apartment!

So then it was time to go to Fish Co. I walk outside + my

> roomates surprised me with a llMO! It was awesome! So we all got to the bar t took a shot and started dancing.
> I looked at my watch at 12:10 to see it was my birthday and I was flinging my arms up t down saying, ITS MY BDAY! I'M 21!

So I got all dolled up, and my friends came over and then we went to Paragon! I got wine there & I was a little drunk. We went back to my room & the pre-game started. Rybo gave me orange rum so I was drinking out of that all nite. It was really awesome having all of my friends at my apartment! So then it was time to go to Fish Co. I walk outside & my roommates surprised me with a limo! It was awesome! So we all go to the bar & took a shot and started dancing. I looked at my watch at 12:10 to see it was my birthday and I was flinging my arms up & down saying it's my bday I'm 21!

I was decked out for my twenty-first birthday. My sister and Nick drove seventeen hours to celebrate with my friends. I was nervous to introduce my friends to Nick. While we were not officially dating, we were very close, and I was honored he wanted to take the trip out to celebrate. Of course, my roommates instantly loved Nick. He gave me matching emerald earrings, a bracelet, and a ring. We kicked off the festivities in our apartment as I played "All You Wanted" by Michelle Branch at least twenty times on repeat (apologies to my sister and friends).

My friends had also surprised me with a limo! We rode in style to the bar where they asked for ID and, for the first time in my life, I showed them *my real* ID. It was so very exciting and liberating. (And now in my forties I get the same amount of excitement when carded).

I must have had at least twenty-one shots, all of which were flushed down the toilet after my stomach did not agree with that amount of alcohol. Besides that trip to the bathroom, I had an amazing twenty-first birthday surrounded by my sister and friends.

May 12, 2002

5-12-02 - My Birthday!
I woke up in pain &
stomach + head hurt,
but it went away
by 3pm. Then I started
packing up, went
to the Olive Garden
(and ordered wine!!) and
then everyone came

over for birthday cake! we left at 2am.

I was sad leaving, but I'm real happy that the year is over. It was a rough year, that I mainly brought on myself. There are some things that I wish I could have changed, but I can only learn from everything now.

I did have fun with my friends, and we all became so much closer because they did give me a tiffanys necklace!

All in all, I'm looking forward to this summer of driving. And being with Nick. Senior year (as scary as it is) will come around soon enough and grant me a new start!

bye! ❀

I woke up in pain, stomach & head hurt but it went away by 3pm. Then I started packing up, went to the Olive Garden (and ordered wine!!) and then everyone came over for birthday cake. We left Providence at 2am. I was sad leaving but I'm real happy that the year is over. It was a rough year that I mainly brought on myself. There are some things that I wish I could have changed but I can only learn from everything now. I did have fun with my friends, and we all became so much closer because they did give me a Tiffany's necklace! All in all, I'm looking forward to this summer of diving. And being with Nick. Senior year (as scary as it is) will come around soon enough and grant me a new start. Bye!

While junior year was thankfully over, it brought me a lot of soul searching. I discovered what I liked, loved, hated, who were my friends, and who I really was. Junior year was scary, painful, and an incredible journey all at once. As much as I hated myself on so many of those days, I am thankful for my experiences. I do not regret my encounters; I learned from them. I was ready to move forward.

Eight days after junior year ended, I found myself at Cedar Point Amusement Park in Sandusky, Ohio.

My mom unwillingly dropped me off at the diving arena (which has since been torn down, sadly). I knew no one. I had only confirmed my availability with the owner, Sean, by phone. My mom surely wanted to bring me home, but I had begged and pleaded with her the entirety of the five-hour drive to Ohio to let me do this. She hesitantly departed, and I was left with my backpack and six new friends. We were instructed to quickly find housing–that same day. A couple of them had already dove summers past and knew the drill. We found a small two-bedroom white house on a corner, conveniently with a bar

165

on the other corner. Two of the divers were dating, so they bunked in the master bedroom. Stef and I shared the other bedroom with our single-sized air mattresses. The room was literally big enough to hold our separate mattresses and the tiny "closet" which barely held our swimsuits, tank tops, and shorts. The other two divers tarped off the living room. And finally, Chris, the professional trampolinist from Texas, lived in the pantry. The pantry was perfectly as big as a single air mattress. He was happy to have a door and just lifted his air mattress during the day so that people could access the pantry. It was fine! When you are twenty-one and living your dream, you do not care about living arrangements.

In the first week at Cedar Point, we learned the show. A man named Bobby flew up from Florida, ensured we understood the plot, rehearsed the skits, and executed the dives. It was a simple twenty-minute show with a voice-over introduction to the main character, who stumbled across a watering hole. He discovered a new world which had pirates trying to get the treasure from the mermaid. The pirates and the mermaid became friends by the end, just as the voice-over from the mermaid proclaimed "The real treasure isn't gold or jewels at all! The real treasure is friendship." The finale showcased one diver who dove from the eighty-foot platform into ten feet of water.

Same show, every single day, five times a day, all summer long, with Tuesdays off. We woke up early and carpooled to the park. We became friends with the workers. They let us jump on the rollercoasters before the park opened. Perks! We ate amusement park food and burned it off during the shows. Twenty minutes of continuous running, climbing up ladders, and diving will do that. We would change things up if it got too monotonous and created different stunts. Shows were performed rain or shine. We all got sick the first week as there was a cold front; we were diving in 58° weather and sometimes in the rain.

Starting the second week of shows, some divers would "get the call" to New York, Atlanta, or other State Fairs and would be gone for a week or longer. I begged to be called for the Taste of Chicago.

About four weeks in, I was summoned to the Illinois State Fair. I was trained to be a mermaid by breathing underwater via scuba gear. At first it was scary not getting full breaths, but they said just take it easy, and I started breathing comfortably. Each pool we dove at had clear glass paneling so you could see the divers' entry into the water, as well as the mermaid emerging from the bottom of the pool to blow kisses and tease the pirates. I officially became *the* mermaid.

I was still waiting every day to get the call for the Taste of Chicago. Management *knew* I wanted it–so there was no reason to ask. I just had to wait.

After being trained as the mermaid, I returned to Ohio and volunteered to be the mermaid during *every* show, which was a welcomed offer. I was given a majestic red tail along with a matching red-sequined bikini top, which was quickly replaced as it was four sizes too big and showed a bit too much. Stef yelled *during* the show "We can see your nips!" I was mortified and wanted to drown. This was a *kid-friendly* show! I was then given a one-piece swimsuit which had flowers sewn on the front; it was an appreciated alternative. The first few shows were hell on my abs. I did, almost, literally drown that first show. The tail was heavy. It would fill with water and was weighed down with scuba diving fins. Try swimming with your feet tied together; it is not easy! The mermaid tail was skintight; I cannot tell you how many times the skin on my left thigh was literally zipped up and then unzipped to free the skin. But this was a show. I was making phenomenal money and most importantly, young girls were watching and looking up to me. I worked with the tail, strengthened my core, and quickly transformed into a mermaid.

We finished our shows each day and headed to the bars for dinner and refreshments. We hit up different bars each night based on their specials. The divers had been doing the show for years and knew everyone at each bar. We worked hard during the day and enjoyed our fun at night. Jägermeister was consumed as frequently as water. A few weeks in, and after a few too many refreshments, one of the seasoned divers, Jimmy Adams, challenged me as to whether I would dive off the thirty-foot platform. I had taken one too many shots of Jägermeister and coyly responded "Of course I can dive off that platform."

To note, prior to joining the circus I had to promise my parents I would not "climb the ladder." Meaning, it was fine to be diving off the ten-foot (three meter) springboard but not off the higher platforms.

The next morning, while I was hoping he had forgotten the conversation, Jimmy entered the pool area. We locked eyes and he yelled, "Climb the ladder!" I nervously and cautiously started climbing the thin medal ladder, hoping he would not see my reservations. I walked to the edge of the small platform and held my breath as I looked down at the pool, thirty feet away. I did a front one and a half somersaults and completed the rotation with fifteen feet to go. My upper back smacked the water, knocked the air out of me, and instantly left welts all down my back. Jimmy yelled, "Get back up there!" I thought he was kidding until I looked at his face. So, I went. There was no other option. I threw the dive again, listened for his call, and nailed the dive. It was thrilling! Jimmy yelled, this time with a smile, "Do it again!" I flew up the ladder with confidence and mastered the dive, as you learn very quickly when diving from those heights. He loved it and we made it a part of the show. I was grateful that Jimmy saw my potential, pushed my boundaries, and coached me through the fun dives.

A week later, my cell phone rang from a number in Florida. It was Sean, the owner, who informed me they needed me at the Taste of Chicago. I got the details I needed and hung up the phone. I must have jumped ten feet in the air, squealed with excitement, and called my parents. Sean wanted Chris—the pantry-living trampolinist—to come to Chicago as well. We packed our bags and drove to Chicago four days later.

I was joined by Chris and five other very talented divers. Sean flew up from Florida to ensure everyone was performing the same skit as in Ohio. We practiced the skit for hours every day and became close friends. Then it was showtime!

Diving in front of thousands of people in my hometown was a dream. As the intro music blasted through the speakers for the first show, my adrenaline and heart were racing. It was simply electrifying.

Two days into our ten-day show, a news team appeared, requested a clip, and instructed anyone who wanted to participate to arrive the next morning at 6:00 a.m. I figured this was the best way to share the news with my parents that I was diving off the thirty-foot platform. The next morning, I called them at 5:58 a.m. and kindly asked them to turn on the news. The news team arrived, interviewed us, and pointed at the helicopter that was taping us. So just as my parents turned on the news, I was climbing up that forbidden ladder with grace. I nailed my front one and a half somersaults while two other divers did front two and a half somersaults below me on the three-meter boards. It looked amazing! (My mother would disagree).

We dove during the day and went out to Chicago's best restaurants and bars at night. We were also fortunate enough to sit on the diving boards during Chicago's stunning 3rd of July firework extravaganza. We literally had the best seats in the house. I invited my sister to hang out with us. After the fireworks, she asked if she could jump in the pool. Sure! I regretted that decision immediately when I remembered she had zero diving experience. She jumped off and nearly hit the edge of the pool. Remind you this pool was 26 feet in diameter and ten feet deep. There is not much room when you jump forward and out. Then the rest of us divers jumped in. Spectators who were walking by thought it was an open pool party and jumped in as well. It quickly became dangerous and very much out of hand. The Chicago Police Department's headquarters were conveniently stationed directly behind the pool. They came rushing in, yelling at everyone to get (the fuck) out of the pool! They circled the tank with flashlights and arrested those who were not part of the diving show. Seconds before, I had grabbed my sister, shoved her into our air-conditioned trailer, and locked her and our beer cooler in the bathroom. I told her to stay there until I let her out. So she sat and she froze. But that was better than her being arrested! Sometime later, after everything calmed down, we fetched her from the bathroom and continued with our night.

I did not want the Taste of Chicago to end. Standing atop the thirty-foot platform and briefly getting a glimpse of the massive crowds sprawling hundreds of yards away was simply exhilarating. There was always a friend or relative at each show who would approach the tank afterwards to say hi just as I had approached it when I was sixteen. It was certainly a dream come true.

Chris and I returned to Ohio. Sean called me again in August, asking if I would be the mermaid at the Minnesota State Fair. I had it down to a science and *loved* being the mermaid. We had even found a bikini top that did not give the crowd an extra show! I was diving alongside six other divers, including Carl Kupper, the coach and diver I had first met at the Taste five years prior.

We headed to the casino our first night in Minnesota. I finally made it to a casino! It must have been after midnight. I found a slot machine, put five dollars in, and won the jackpot. Alarms were going off. I called my parents and excitedly told them the news. I lost track of the time, woke them up, and while they were happy for me, reminded me of the late hour, told me to save a hundred dollars, and have fun with the rest.

The most upsetting day in Minnesota occurred three days later. There was a tiny wooden box (called the mermaid box) atop the back of the stage where I would slip my shimmering gold tail on and off (I wore a well-fitted bikini underneath). I would drape the tail over a ladder so it would dry between shows and then climb down the ladder to the backstage area and join the rest of the divers. So, as I did every day, I unzipped and removed the tail, stepped down, and came face to face with a five-year-old girl with blond hair donning adorable pigtails. She had managed to walk around the backstage area. We locked eyes and her jaw dropped. She cried out "I thought you were a *real* mermaid!" Her eyes filled with tears. I quickly reminded her that mermaids get legs when they are out of the water. She did not buy it for a second. Apparently, she had not seen *The Little Mermaid*. She started sobbing and walked back to her mother, who gave me a look. I still see that little girl's face when I think about Minnesota.

At the end of the summer, I got the call for the California State Fair. I would have missed my first day of senior year–which is not a big deal. People switch classes, people change out; *it is not a big deal.* But my parents thought it was a *GIANT* deal and shut down any thoughts of me going to California. Maybe because the circus mentioned they also wanted me to be the mermaid in Rio de Janeiro, which followed the California State Fair. I am convinced my life would have taken an interesting turn should I have gone to the California State Fair. It is humorous, looking back, how many times my parents were right when I wanted them to be so wrong. But at the end of the day, they were just wanting the best for their daughter, including, but not limited to, a college degree, which sadly cannot be obtained while being a mermaid in Rio de Janeiro.

SENIOR YEAR

6

BLANK SLATE

September 3, 2002

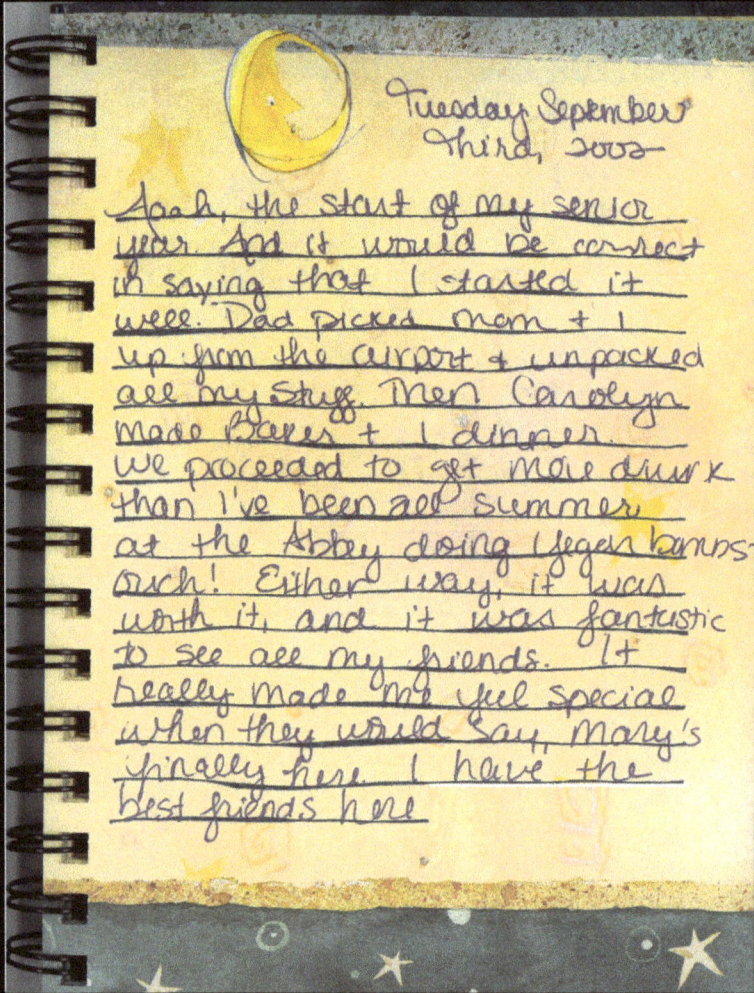

Tuesday September Third, 2002

Aaah, the start of my senior year. And it would be correct in saying that I started it well. Dad picked mom + I up from the airport & unpacked all my stuff. Then Carolyn made Baker + I dinner. We proceeded to get more drunk than I've been all summer, at the Abbey doing Vegas bombs—ouch! Either way, it was worth it, and it was fantastic to see all my friends. It really made me feel special when they would say, Mary's finally here. I have the best friends here

Aaah the start of my senior year. And it would be correct in saying that I started it well. Dad picked up Mom & I up from the airport and unpacked all my stuff. Then Carolyn made Baker & I dinner. We proceeded to get more drunk than I've been all summer at the Abbey doing Jaeger bombs – ouch! Either way, it was worth it, and it was fantastic to see all my friends. It really made me feel special when they would say, Mary's finally here! I have the best friends here!

Oh, it was so great to be back. Although I was in slight disbelief it was my final year, I was ready to be reunited with my girlfriends. I had experienced many things and finally felt in control with navigating my own ship again. I was determined to make the most of every day. We picked up right where we left off. I had a fresh start and the best friends a girl could ask for. I was doing great academically and entered into my final year of diving.

What could possibly go wrong?

September 8, 2002

Sunday September 8

I woke up early &
Carolyn + I met Meredith
at the Red Sox game. It
was really good to see
them after there last trip
here to the East coast.
The Red Sox ended up losing
but then dad & mom turn
my roomates & me out to
Hemonways. We had a
real great time. Then they
left, & Carolyn, Kim +
I went to Pats Pub + did
Karaoke- lemme tell you
how much fun it was!
I got back to my room -
and hick left me an

I M. So I called him & we had - what I thought - such a nice, normal conversation, and I got out everything I wanted to. I don't blame him - but he had no sympathy or feelings for me. I pronounced my love for him, and he had no response. I'm hoping all it will take is time. In my heart I'd love to be back with him, but in his head, he has no reason to be back with me.

I woke up early & Carolyn & I met Mom and Dad at the Red Sox game. It was really good to see them after [their] last trip here to the East Coast. The Red Sox ended up losing but then dad and mom took my roommates & me out to Hemingways. We had a real great time. Then they left, & Carolyn, Kim & I went to Pat's Pub & did karaoke — lemme tell you how much fun it was! I got back to my room- and Nick left me an IM. So I called him and we had — what I thought — such a nice, normal conversation and I got out everything I wanted to. I don't blame him — but he had no sympathy or feelings for me. I pronounced my love for him and he had no response. I'm hoping all it will take is time. In my heart I'd love to be back with him, but in his head, he has no reason to be back with me.

September 9, 2002

Monday, September 9th

What a great day! I walked
over to skiing. I never walked
in & decided to take us
water skiing! Me, Jamie, Abby
(the new driver), & neverr
family all went! I wish
I would have had a camera
because it was so hilarious.
I ended up getting right up,
and tried to slalom. We even
had webby's for dinner!!
    But then I got home &
talked to Nick. Hes real mad
about me not including him
in my Summer. But why
Should I? i'm young & I
shouldn't relinquish my

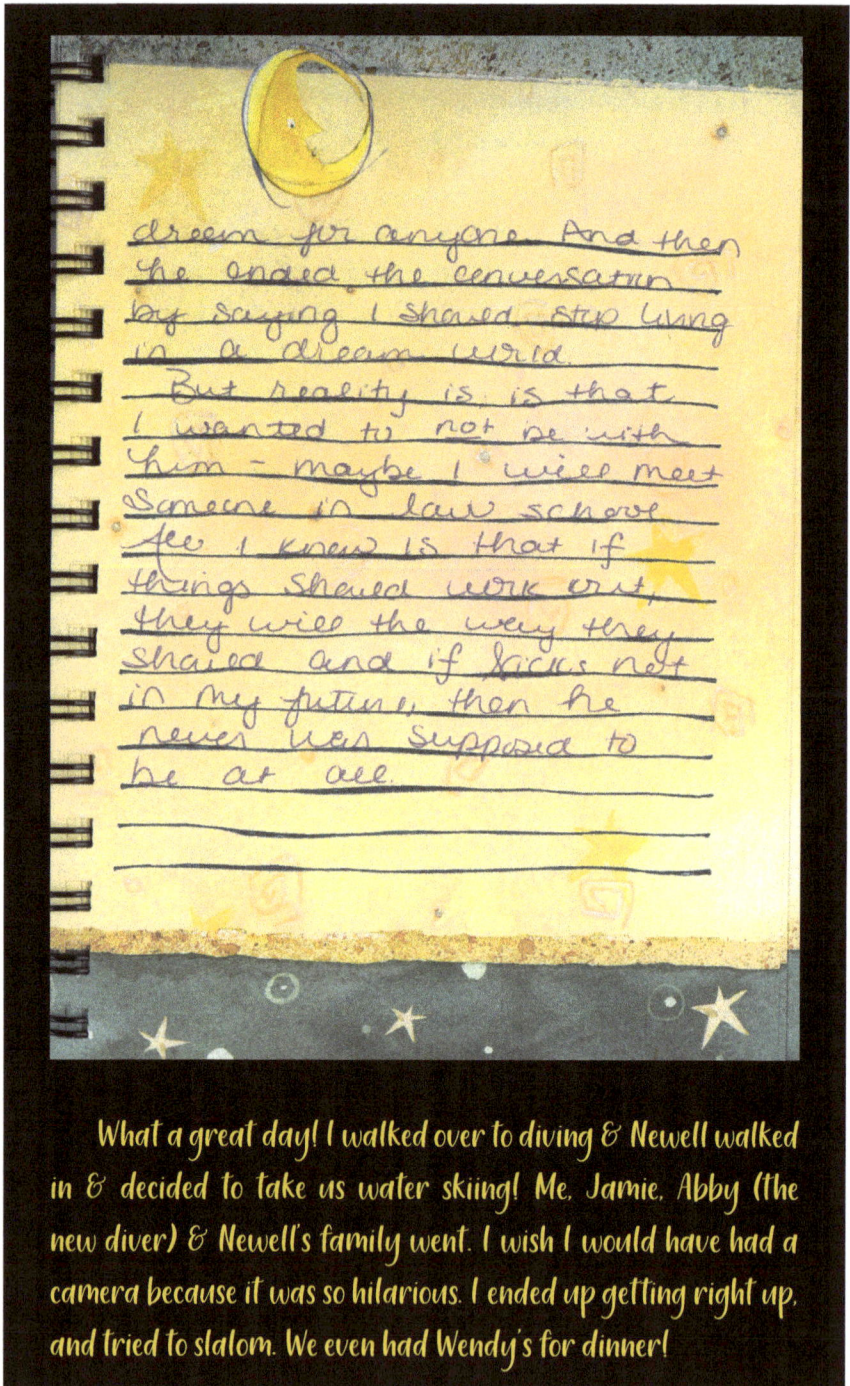

dream for anyone. And then he ended the conversation by saying I should stop living in a dream world.

But reality is, is that I wanted to not be with him — maybe I will meet someone in law school too. I knew is that if things should work out, they will the way they should and if he's not in my future, then he never was supposed to be at all.

What a great day! I walked over to diving & Newell walked in & decided to take us water skiing! Me, Jamie, Abby (the new diver) & Newell's family went. I wish I would have had a camera because it was so hilarious. I ended up getting right up, and tried to slalom. We even had Wendy's for dinner!

> But then I got home & talked to Nick. He's real mad about me not including him in my summer but why should I? I'm young & I shouldn't relinquish my dream for anyone. And then he ended the conversation by saying I should stop living in a dream world.
>
> But reality is is that I wanted to not be with him – maybe I will meet someone in law school. All I know is that if things should work out, they will the way they should and if Nick's not in my future, then he never was supposed to be at all.

The second I fully immersed myself back on the East Coast, Nick never failed to enter my life. This last summer was spent with the All-American High Dive Team. The problem was, when we traveled to the Taste of Chicago, I was halfway through the summer and fully engaged with my diving crew. Nick wanted to hang out. He could not understand why I did not spend time with him, away from the after-show dinners and events with the divers. This was my dream and I was fully vested. The circus put us up (for free) at amazing hotels. No one ever paid for a fancy hotel room for me. I was raised knowing if you want something, you need to work for it, and I had worked *really* hard to be here. I wanted to stay at fancy hotels with the divers and literally enjoy every second. I did my best to balance the circus life with my reality, but it was hard.

Nick did not get it and I did not feel like explaining it. Nick also wanted to join me at the Minnesota State Fair. I put my foot down and said no. He did not take it well at all. I understood why he was upset; our summers were our time to hang out. But he also knew I had chosen the circus over him. The circus was my dream, ever since I was sixteen years old, not his. When he did not understand, it upset me and ultimately ended our relationship.

You know the saying "If you love something, let it go. If it returns, it is yours; if it doesn't, it wasn't." I believed in this saying. Literally believing it was real, I challenged it. Not only challenged it, I burned Nick. Broke him. Broke us. And stupidly and ignorantly thought, maybe he will come back–that is what the saying is, right? He did not wait for me; he did not return. It was probably for the best. In those first few weeks of senior year, I was still stupidly hoping, waiting and wanting things to change.

Certainly, I do regret hurting him. I am positive he moved on and found a wonderful person to spend the rest of his life with, as did I. But the hurt I caused him was cruel and unintentional. It was a perfectly imperfect relationship which was over, and I navigated on without him. The bottom line is when it was convenient for me to be hanging out with him, we would shine. And when it was not the best time, I would push him away. That is not love. It just would have been kinder to walk away in the beginning than to drag him through the mud. I just really did not know any better.

September 10, 2002

I attended my last NCAA compliance meeting. It's kinda sad cuz this is the beginning of the end for me. Then I went diving, and Melissa had dinner ready when I got back!

It was taking some time for me to digest this was my last year in college. It was the start of many endings, such as the last NCAA Compliance meeting. I looked around the room and easily spotted the eager wide-eyed freshman, intently listening to the moderators, exactly how I must have looked four years prior. I learned to enjoy the moment.

September 18, 2002

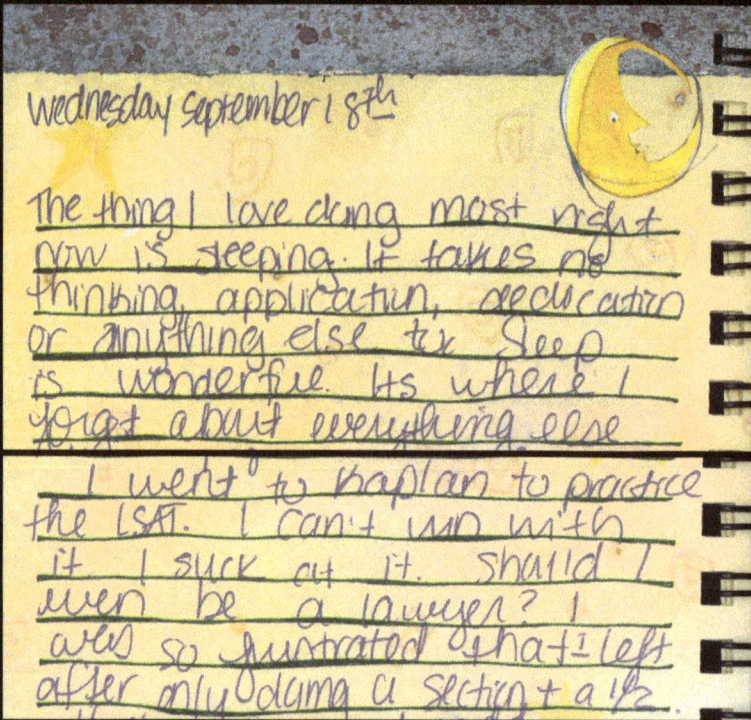

wednesday september 18th

The thing I love doing most right now is sleeping. It takes no thinking, application, dedication or anything else to. Sleep is wonderful. Its where I forgot about everything else

I went to kaplan to practice the LSAT. I can't win with it. I suck at it. Should I even be a lawyer? I was so funtrated that I left after only doing a section + a 1/2

The thing I love doing most right now is sleeping. It takes no thinking, application, dedication or anything else to. Sleep is wonderful. It's where I forget about everything else. I went to Kaplan to practice the LSAT. I can't win with it. I suck at it. Should I even be a lawyer? I was so frustrated that I left after only doing a section & a 1/2.

Reality was starting to sink in. The Law School Admissions Test (LSAT) was approaching, and I was exhausted thinking about it. Surely, this is a time in my life where I wish I could hit the rewind button, switch gears, and head into something that excited, not frustrated, me. But at the time, I was a senior in college choosing a path based upon what I thought I wanted to do in the future–and I (incorrectly) thought I *had* to stick with that path.

Remember this: you are free to change your mind. A year and a half later, after I had finished a full year of law school, I dropped out–it was not for me. And to this day, I do not regret that decision, not even a tiny bit. I am grateful I had the law school experience and came to that decision on my own. The lesson I am trying to get across is that it is *okay to change your mind.* What you declare your major will be, or simply what you want to do with your life *can change.*

September 20, 2002

Friday September 20th

I woke up at 10:20 for my 10:30 class but I still went. Diving was ok – I signed up to get a massage at the trainer for Monday. Then tonite was senior nite – and it was a real good time – I was finally legally allowed in the beer garden + all the seniors were there. The hockey players were there, a couple even said hi, but I blatently ignored them

I woke up at 10:20 for my 10:30 class but I still went. Diving was ok – I signed up to get a massage at the trainer for Monday. Then tonite was Senior nite – and it was a real good time – I was finally legally allowed in the beer garden & all the seniors were there. The hockey players were there, a couple even said hi, but I blatantly ignored them.

What is humorous to me is that the instant I decided it was not in my best interest to pursue any of the hockey players, they started initiating the conversations. But I had determined through my own experience sophomore year and through rumors junior year that it was *not* in my best interest to pursue these appealing athletes. Make up your own mind about who you are spending your extra time with and always go with your gut.

September 22, 2002

Sunday Sept. 22

well I went ahead + bought Nick (+ Kathy) a bday present but I don't know if I should send it to him- hes not talking to me.

On a better note, I raised my LSAT score by 9 points on the practice test. AND Carole said shed write me a letter of recommendation! tonite, Baker, Carolyn + I went to Karaoke. It was so much fun once again. I sang a bunch + got applause, but I kept thinking about Nick the whole time. I need to get over him.

Well, I went ahead & bought Nick (& Kathy) a bday present but I don't know if I should send it to him — he's not talking to me.

> On a better note, I raised my LSAT score by 9 points on the practice test, AND Carol [redacted] said she'd write me a letter of recommendation!
>
> Tonite, Baker, Carolyn & I went to karaoke. It was so much fun once again. I sang a bunch & got applauded, but I kept thinking about Nick the whole time. I need to get over him.

Most of my fondest memories senior year include karaoke nights with Baker and Carolyn. Baker (her college nickname that stuck)—and I lived in the same hallway sophomore year. We hung out with the same mutual friends and then discovered we had way too much in common to not be best friends. She invited me to her twentieth birthday party, and we became lifelong friends who hung out regularly.

We found a pub nearby that offered karaoke on Sunday nights. The three of us just had so much fun. None of us were very good at singing, although the more we drank, the more we turned into rockstars. I also found the more I drank, the more I thought of Nick. I just could not get him out of my head. I wanted to be a part of his life but that had not worked, nor would it. I could not commit to a long-distance relationship, nor was he asking me for that. And then at karaoke that night, my girlfriend asserted "The best way to get over someone is to get under someone else." My inner Catholic school girl was mortified, but my drunken self was intrigued.

September 30, 2002

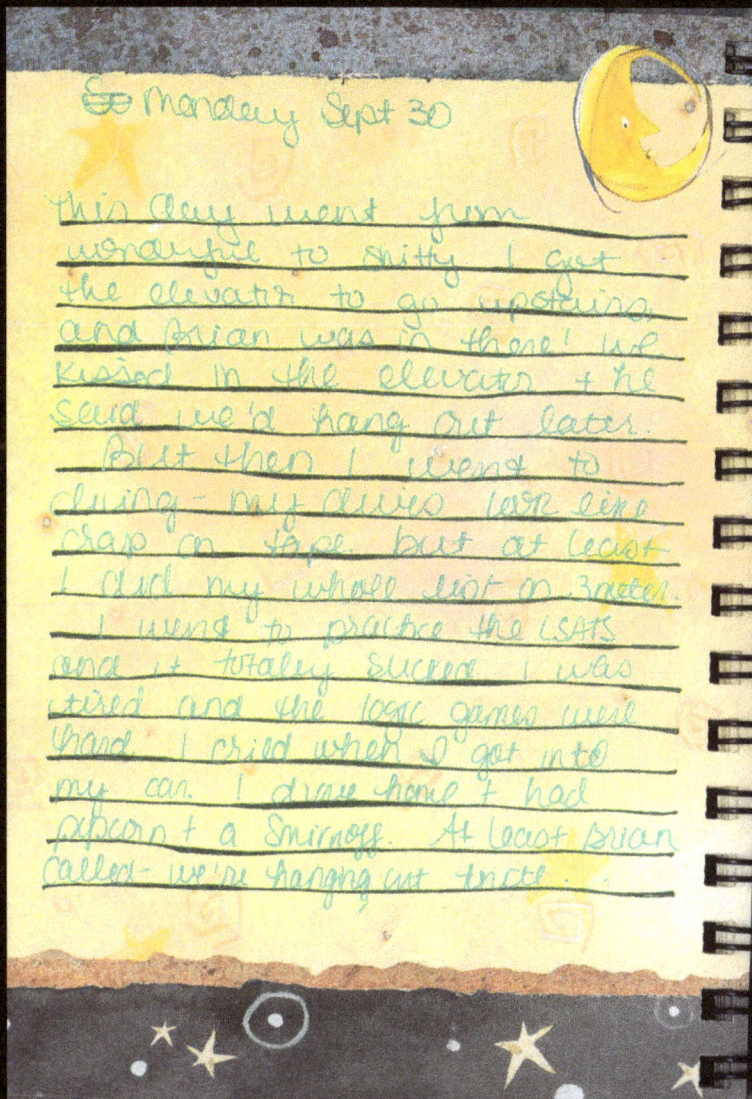

Monday Sept 30

This day went from wonderful to shitty. I got the elevator to go upstairs and Brian was in there! We kissed in the elevator + he said we'd hang out later. But then I went to dubbing - my dubs are like crap on tape. but at least I did my whole list in 3 weeks. I went to practice the LSATS and it totaly sucked. I was tired and the logic games were hard. I cried when I got into my car. I drove home + had popcorn + a Smirnoff. At least Brian called - we're hanging out tmrw.

This day went from wonderful to shitty. I got the elevator
to go upstairs and Brian was in there! We kissed in the elevator

& he said we'd hang out later. But then I went diving – my dives looked like crap on tape. But at least I did my whole list on 3 meter. I went to practice the LSATs and it totally sucked. I was tired and the logic games were hard. I cried when I got into my car. I drove home and had popcorn and a Smirnoff. At least Brian called, we're hanging out tonite.

I had decided over the summer I would primarily focus on my friendships senior year. I was not looking for a relationship. I just wanted to enjoy time with my friends as I knew I would be moving home after college, halfway across the country from these amazing girls. Brian had re-emerged. Why we always seemed to run into each other in the elevator is beyond me. The elevator door opened, and there was Brian again, standing with the same million-dollar smile as he did junior year. And I fell for it, again. Brian was truly just a wonderful placeholder in my heart for Nick. He was the temporary fix I needed. But he ended up messing with my heart and my mind more than I could have ever imagined.

October 5, 2002

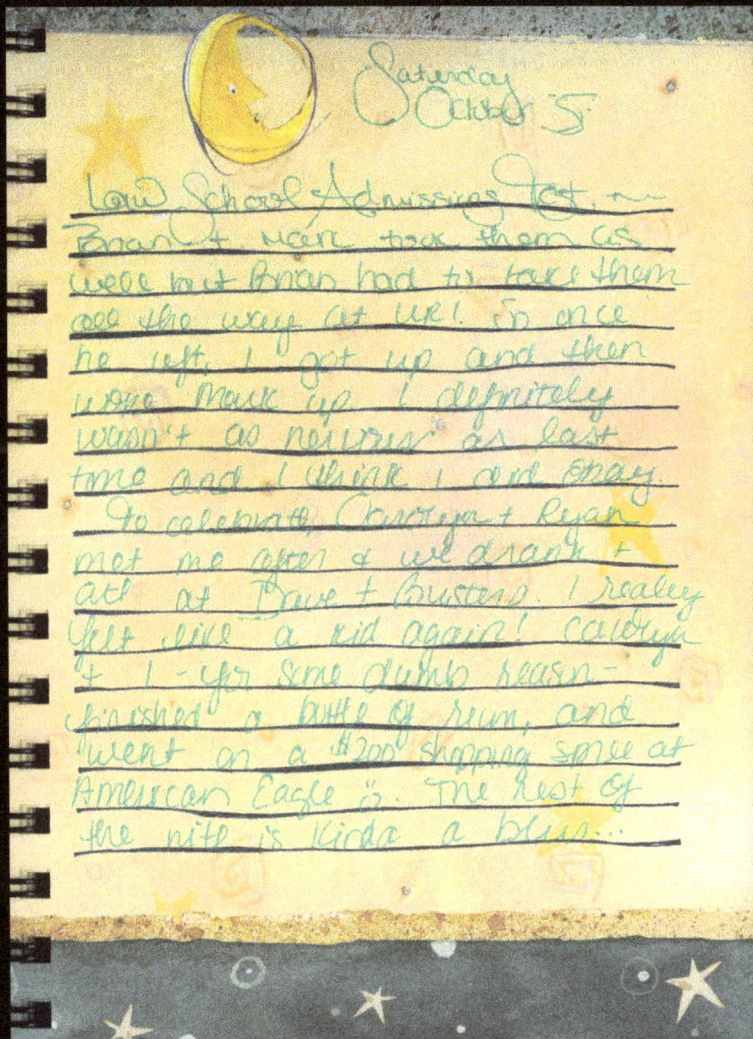

Law School Admissions Test — Brian & Mark took them as well but Brian had to take them all the way at URI. So once he left, I got up and then woke Mark up. I definitely wasn't as nervous as last time and I think I did okay. To celebrate, Carolyn & Ryan met me after & we drank & ate at Dave & Busters. I really felt like a kid again! Carolyn & I — for some dumb reason — finished a bottle of rum and went on a $200 shopping spree at American Eagle. The rest of the nite is kinda a blur...

Today was the day. It was the Law School Admissions Test. I slept well, ate a good breakfast, and was fully prepared to take this test. I was certainly nervous but knew I had to do my absolute best. No pressure, right? I took my time completing the questions and before I knew it, time was up. I handed in the papers, not knowing whether I did okay or not. I had to wait six long weeks for the results. Completing this test caused me to initiate a rewards/benefit system. Have a hard day? Treat yourself at night. Lose some weight? Get a new workout outfit. It seems innocent until you start adding alcohol. Take a law school admissions test? Drink an entire bottle of rum. Balance and moderation are certainly needed, but hard to practice when it comes to the extremes.

October 21, 2002

Weekend of october 21st

By far the coolest weekend~ on Saturday after going to sleep at 4am on Friday after the fall festival, we hopped on a bus to NYC! Dana was pointing everything out as we drove by & it was amazing. We walked thru times square and went to lunch. Then we saw Rent on Broadway, which was unbelievable. We went to a real good pizza place and then took the subway to Mike + Kim. There place is so cool! And they were so nice. They sat us right down and had a drink w/ us. We started to get ready & Mike, Dana + I went to the alcohol store. Then Mike + Kim took us into a bar in Times Square. It was very

fun. Mike + I did shots together and
it was really awesome dancing
& partying with them. We were
all wasted at 3am when we
left & when we walked outside,
Mike signaled down a TAXI for us! It
was so cool! I stood up thru the
sunroof while we were cruising thru
NYC. It felt awesome. The girls passed
out when we got back to the house
but Mike + his friend Blair took
me up to the 7th story. Mike said,
"Mary Ellen - welcome to new York city"
I've never been as hungry as
I was the next day, but it
was definitely worth it. It
was the coolest weekend!

By far the coolest weekend – on Saturday – after going to sleep at 4am on Friday after the Fall Festival, we hopped on a bus to NYC! Dana was pointing everything out as we drove by & it was amazing. We walked thru Times Square and went to lunch. Then we saw Rent on Broadway which was unbelievable. We went to a real good pizza place and then took the subway to Mike & Kims. Their place is so cool! And they were so nice. They sat us right down and had a drink w/ us. We started to get ready & Mike, Dana & I went to the alcohol store. Then Mike & Kim took us into a bar in Times Square. It was very fun. Mike & I did shots together and it was really awesome bonding & partying with them. We were all wasted at 3am when we left & when we walked outside Mike signaled a TAXI for us! It was so cool! I stood up thru the sunroof while we were driving thru NYC. It felt awesome. The girls passed out when we got back to the house but Mike & his friend Blain[e] took me up to the 7th story. Mike said "Mary Ellen – Welcome to New York City." I've never been as hungover as I was the next day, but it was definitely worth it. It was the coolest weekend!

New York City, and chauffeured around by one of my favorite cousins, Mike. Remember the introduction regarding my Irish Catholic family? That means I have fourteen first cousins–twenty-eight after the Irish weddings. Mike takes any party to the next level. He finds his way into the inner circles, rubbing shoulders with celebrities. He has attended the most amazing parties and was somehow present in the Blackhawks locker room getting champagne dumped over his head during the Stanley Cup Championship. His stories and tales of his adventures are endless. I have always looked up to Mike and could not wait to party with him in New York City!

Dana, Melissa, Kristen and I were excited for our trip to New York and crashed at Mike's apartment. After we hit up a handful of his favorite bars, downing more shots than I can remember and dancing with my girlfriends, Mike–in true Mike style–flagged down a limo for us girls. We did not hesitate to stand up through the open sunroof while we excitedly giggled and waved our arms around, smack dab in the middle of New York City. The cool night air hit our hands in return as we drove through Times Square. I was immersed in this amazing city and epic night!

After we returned to his apartment, the girls found whatever sleeping spot they could (including the bathtub), while Mike, his friend Blaine, and I continued drinking. They took me up to the rooftop. I stepped from the super steep staircase onto the rooftop and lost my breath at the view. Skyscrapers and buildings lit up the night sky. Car horns echoed through the streets. Even at 4:00 a.m., the city was alive. We talked about our family and our night in the city until the sun started to rise. We had such an unforgettable trip to New York and I was lucky to experience it with my roommates and cousin!

October 31, 2002

Thursday
October 31 Halloween!

I was afraid for today cuz
each Halloween gets progessively
worse. but this Halloween rocked
All 8 of us dressed up as
Rockstars w/ red shorts & baseball
jerseys. We all had nicknames
& numbers on the back w/
TUBE socks! I was so excited
to wear them! I was pretty
drunk as we headed out &
It was a blast when we
got there. I talked to a lot
of random guys but when
I got home. I made a huge
mistake. I IMed Nick & told
him that I still love him
Yea the problem is is that

197

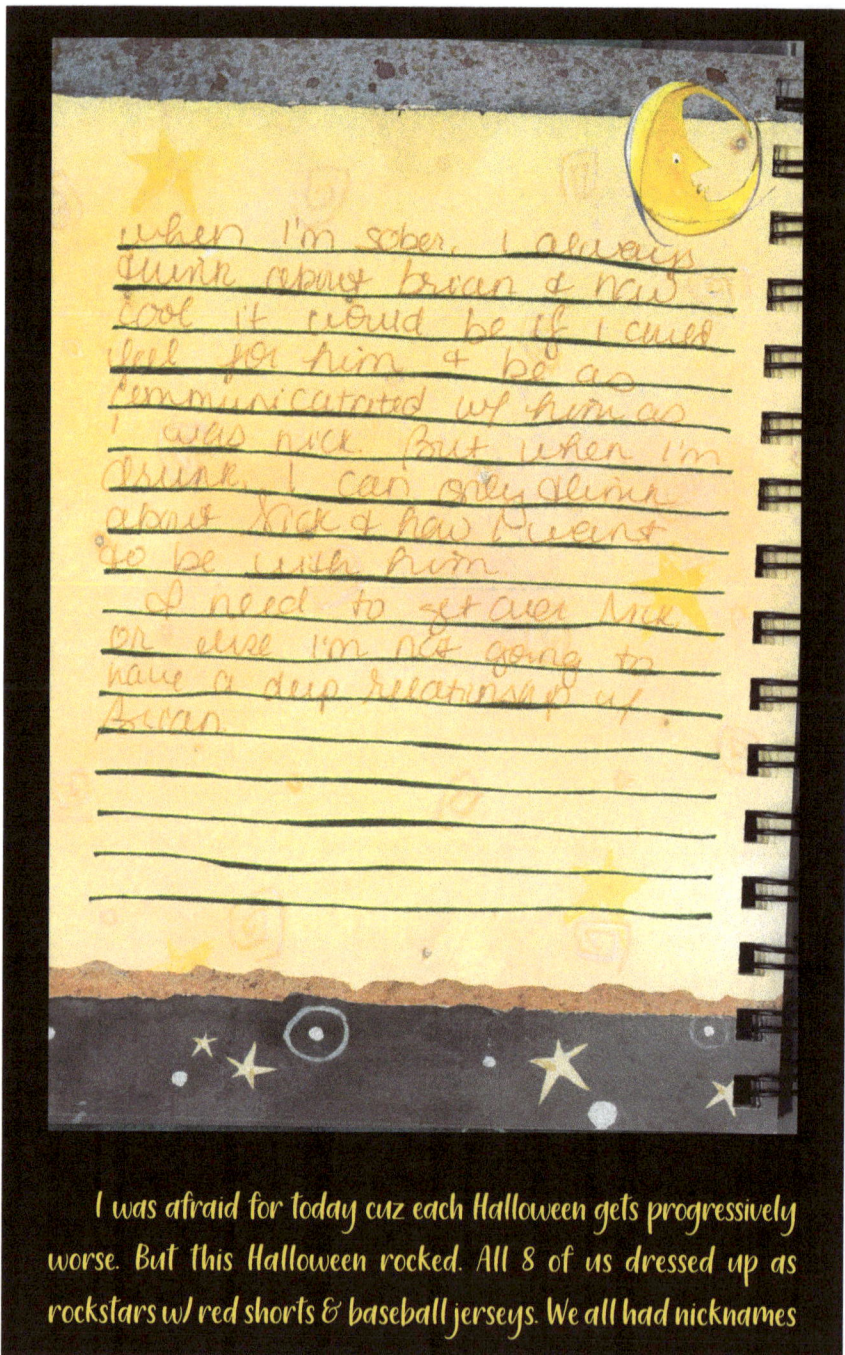

when I'm sober, I always think about brian & how cool it would be if I cried feel for him & be as communicated w/ him as I was nice. But when I'm drunk, I can only think about Nick & how I want to be with him

I need to get over Nick or else I'm not going to have a deep relationship w/ brian

I was afraid for today cuz each Halloween gets progressively worse. But this Halloween rocked. All 8 of us dressed up as rockstars w/ red shorts & baseball jerseys. We all had nicknames

& numbers on the back with TUBE SOCKS! I was so excited to wear them! I was pretty drunk as we headed out & it was a blast when we got there. I talked to a lot of random guys but when I got home I made a huge mistake. I IMed Nick & told him that I still love him. Yea. The problem is is that when I'm sober I always think about Brian and how cool it would be if I could feel for him & be as communicated w/ him as I was Nick. But when I'm drunk, I can only think about Nick & how I want to be with him. I need to get over Nick or else I'm not going to have a deep relationship w/ Brian.

Senior year Halloween night was the *best* Halloween I had in college. We were truly rock stars. I cherished that night with my best girlfriends.

I honestly wish I could have told my twenty-year-old self to stop caring and worrying about guys–that all got figured out when I was much older and wiser. Enjoy your rock star nights. They do not last forever.

November 8, 2002

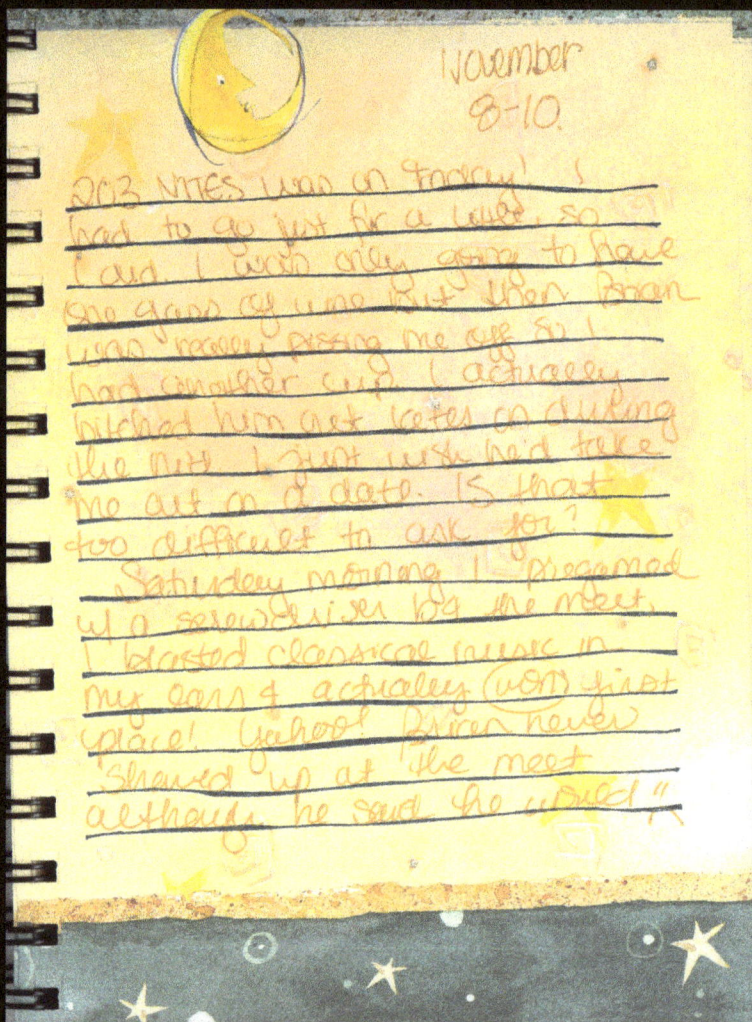

203 Nites was on Friday! I had to go just for a little, so I did. I was only going to have one glass of wine but then Brian was really pissing me off so I had another cup. I actually bitched

him out later on during the nite. I just wish he'd take me out on a date. Is that too difficult to ask for? Saturday morning I pregamed with a screwdriver before the meet. I blasted classical music in my ears & actually won first place! Yahoo! Brian never showed up at the meet although he said he would.

203 nights was the party to "celebrate" the fact that we only had 203 nights before graduation. While I wanted to attend, I had a diving meet the next morning and knew I could not stay long. There was actually a reason Brian was acting so foolish which was revealed to me within the coming days.

In the meantime, and as said before, please do not settle for anyone treating you less than what you are worth. **Do not lessen your value for someone else**. I was being tolerated instead of being celebrated. And not only did Brian disregard me that night, he promised and then failed to show at my diving meet. If I had just ended it then, I would have saved so much heartbreak.

November 12, 2002

Tuesday November 12

Kim Baker came over tonite. She closed
my door + said Mary i have to tell
you something. She told me that
Brian had been seeing this other girl
for 2 months as well. I asked
her to leave + sobbed uncontrollable.
i had to call her to find out if its
true. So I called her up and she
had just found out as well at 203
nights. So I went over there
so we could plan on him coming
over, as he did. He wouldn't
get out of his car, so I went
out there, and the look on
his face said it all. He got
caught big time. He made me
stand out in the rain while

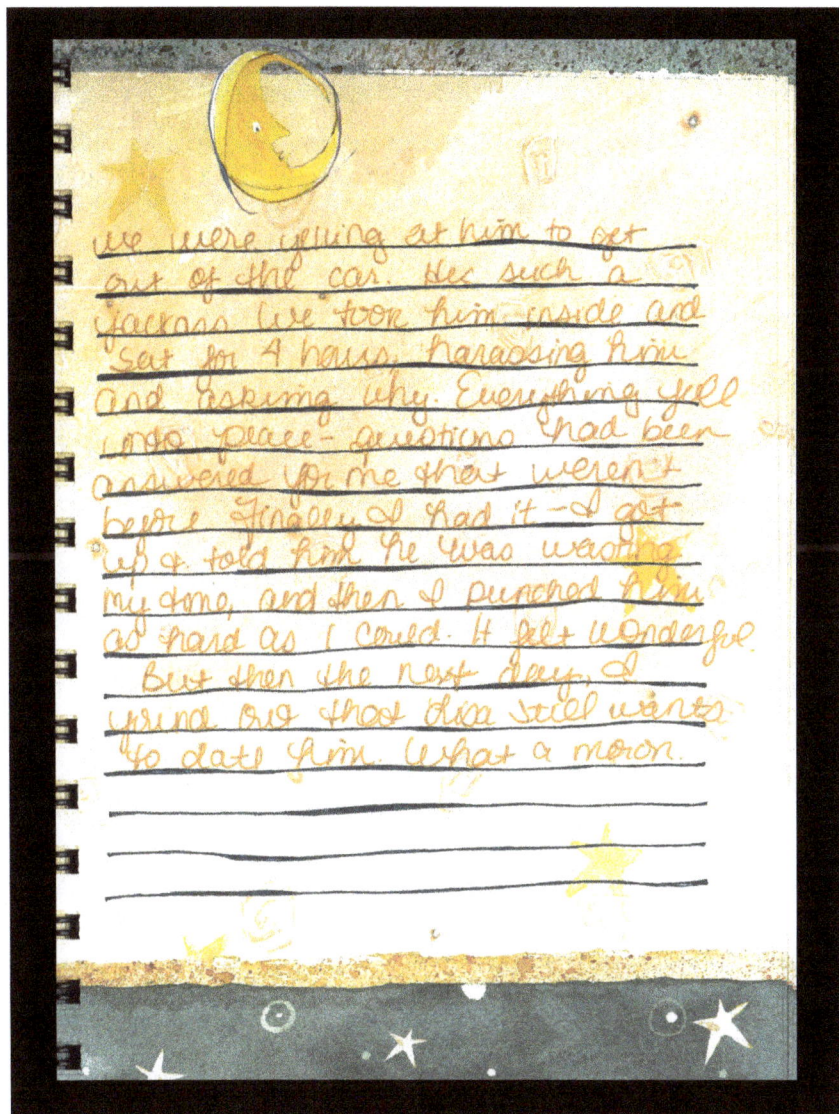

we were yelling at him to get
out of the car. He's such a
jackass we took him inside and
sat for 4 hours, harassing him
and asking why. Everything yell
into peace - questions had been
answered for me that weren't
before. Finally I had it - I got
up & told him he was wasting
my time, and then I punched him
as hard as I could. It felt wonderful.
But then the next day, I
found out that Lisa still wants
to date him. What a moron.

Kim Baker came over tonite. She closed my door & said Mary I have to tell you something. She told me that Brian had been seeing this Lisa girl for 2 months as well. I asked her to leave & sobbed uncontrollably. I had to call her to find out if its true. So I called her up and she had just found out as well at 203 nights. So I went over there so we could plan on him coming over, as he did. He wouldn't get out of his car. So I went out there and the look on his face said it all. He got caught big time. He made me stand out in the rain while we were yelling at him to get out of the car. He's such a jackass. We took him inside and sat for 4 hours, harassing him and asking why. Everything fell into place – questions had been answered for me that weren't before. Finally, I had it – I got up & told him he was wasting my time, and then I punched him as hard as I could. It felt wonderful. But then the next day, I found out that Lisa still wants to date him. What a moron.

To say I was caught by surprise would be an understatement. Baker had informed me Brian was dating *both* Lisa and me. I had to confront all of this immediately. I called Lisa, and we were both friendly and sympathetic towards each other. We wanted to talk further, and she invited me over to her off-campus apartment. When I arrived at Lisa's, we literally went through every weekend in our calendars for the last two months. Every weekend he was short with me and/or ignored me were the weekends he was with Lisa. And vice versa. And it all concluded with 203 nights, when he was there, with *Lisa*. It now made sense why he was ignoring me that night. We decided it would be humorous to call Brian over to her house. Certainly, he did not know I was there.

Lisa and I were standing outside ready to greet him as he pulled into the driveway. It was pouring. His face turned a shade of ghost-white and he cowardly refused to get out of his car. We yelled at him through the windows for twenty minutes and finally, he begrudgingly got out of his car. After hours of ugly confrontation, I was ready to leave. I had never hit anyone in my life. It was a mere impulse to punch him as hard as I possibly could, and it felt *amazing*. Baker and I left that toxic house and headed out to the bars to celebrate my newfound single status. I was a little surprised when Lisa coyly stated she wanted to stay with Brian and stick it out. I had never felt so sorry for another human being, and personally so foolish and defeated. I vowed it would never happen again.

I pray you never encounter the emotions I felt that day. It was certainly liberating and clarifying getting the answers I was searching for, but I invested way too much time into this person who hurt me so badly. I trusted him too much.

It took me many, many years to heal those wounds and start again. It is hard putting yourself out there after heartbreak–it surely does not happen overnight–nor should it. It takes confidence, work, strength and good friends by your side.

I closed the door to future relationships senior year. I had enough.

* * *

I turned the page in my journal.

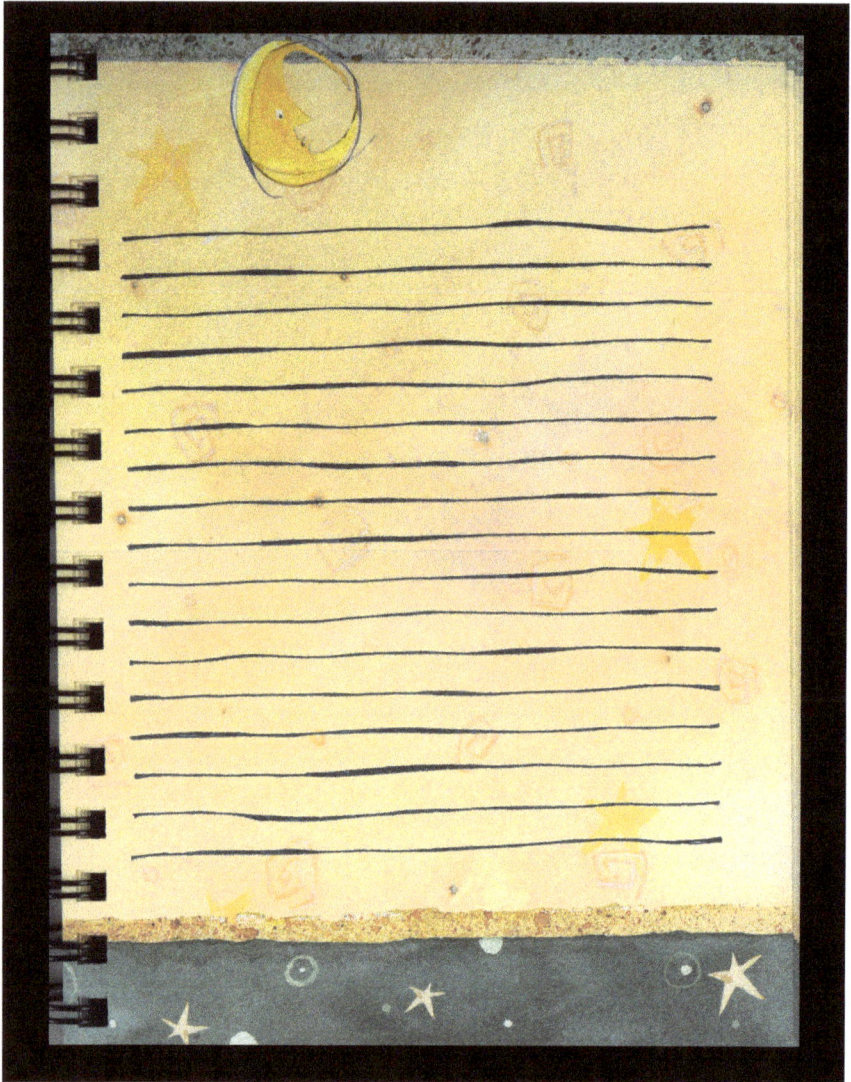

To my dismay, the journal entry was blank. My entire second semester of senior year was undocumented. I had stopped writing—maybe because I did not want college to end or because I did not have the perfect ending.

I was not ready to write my ending because, frankly, I did not know what it was. Aren't we all still trying to figure that out?

Please do not waste your days. Make each day purposeful and meaningful. Write that ending and live it out. Make your plan–your roadmap–because if there is nothing moving you towards a better ending, then what are you really doing?

* * *

While not documented, both the swimming and diving teams headed to the University of Hawaii for the winter training trip. It was wonderful having both teams together. We had a blast exploring the islands. After not qualifying for the BIG EAST my junior year, I worked incredibly hard to ensure I did qualify senior year. I finished my diving career on a high note at the Championship Meet. I made it to finals on both the 1- and 3-meter boards and could not have wished for a better meet, witnessed by my parents. It was certainly bittersweet. My diving career had come full circle. All the time, commitments, practices, and sacrifices I made in high school and college were worth it.

If you can partake in collegiate sports, *please* do so. You may be astonished by the amount of drinking that was documented during my college years, but you should know that behind the scenes, just as much schoolwork was also being done. In order to remain on the swimming and diving team, one must maintain a certain GPA. If it is not maintained, you are kicked off the team. I witnessed it during my freshman year, which instilled a fear that carried with me all four years. Balancing academic and personal priorities takes an extraordinary amount of dedication and discipline, but becoming a four-year Academic All American made the commitment worth it. You will have lifelong friendships with your teammates. I would also highly suggest *not* selecting a school *just* for the sport–I had a friend who received a full diving scholarship. Five weeks into practice, she broke her ankle which ended her diving career. She lost the scholarship and ended up transferring as she had solely picked the school for diving. Certainly, there are arguments for both sides; at the end of the day, you need to pick what is best for you. Follow your gut!

While I planned on skating through music classes my final semester, Sister Gail had other plans for me. Baker and I had both registered for Piano 101. We were going to take it together as we thought it would be fun. On the first day of class, Sister Gail approached me and said you are *not* taking Piano 101. I tried telling her I needed to brush up on the basics, but she did not believe me for a second. Poor Baker was left to take piano on her own, an instrument she had never played. Sister Gail suggested I take a composition class. It was the most challenging yet rewarding class I had ever taken. For the final, we had to compose and perform our own original song. I was pushed way outside of my comfort zone but enjoyed performing my original song for my classmates. I would strongly suggest expanding your boundaries with your classes and hope you do not regret it.

I graduated with honors on May 18, 2003.

My roommates and I could not fathom college ending, so we extended the party for three additional months. We found a very cute beach house in Narragansett and signed a summer lease. We all had easy day jobs, which warranted just enough money for groceries and bar tabs. We had the best parties. I would highly recommend doing this if you are ever presented with the opportunity. Life can wait; the chances of being able to partake in adventures quickly diminish after college!

My sister flew from Chicago and joined me in Narragansett on the last day of our lease to accompany me on the long drive home.

I cried as we left the place that provided me a home for four very short years, lifelong friends, beautiful coast lines, and a funny accent.

ACKNOWLEDGMENTS

Thank you to Publish Your Purpose, Jenn T. Grace, Chris Agnos, and the rest of the team for believing in my book and making this all possible.

Thank you to my husband, Garrett, who has been my soundboard since day one. I love you and JD for being by my side and supporting my dreams and goals.

Thank you to my parents, Dennis and Carol. Thank you for believing in me, allowing me to spread my wings and experience everything college had to offer. Thank you to my brother and sister for being the best siblings and for leading the way.

Thank you to my lifelong college friends who were my cheerleaders and support system - specifically, Ryan, Carolyn, Baker and Kate. I would not have the confidence to move forward without you by my side.

Thank you to my cousin Michael for your infinite wisdom and encouragement. To Joel Hoekstra, for your inspiration, to Jimmy Adams, for taking me under your wing when I landed in Ohio and showing me the ropes. To Daniela, for your observation, deskside pep talks and marketing wisdom. And to Elise and Madi, thank you for your love and support. I hope you have your best four years at college!

And finally, to Aja Volkman. Your interest in my book was the motivation I needed to complete it. And my idol, Lady Gaga, for your acceptance speech during your Oscar win for Shallow. Your words hit me on another level, which I will share with you here:

And if you are at home, and you're sitting on your couch and you're watching this right now, all I have to say is that this is hard work. I've worked hard for a long time, and it's not about winning. But what it's about is not giving up. If you have a dream, fight for it. There's a discipline for passion. And it's not about how many times you get rejected or you fall down or you're beaten up. It's about how many times you stand up and are brave and you keep on going.

ABOUT THE AUTHOR

Mary Reid studied History and Music in College, traveled the country with the All-American High Dive Team, dabbled in Law School and currently works as a paralegal at a prestigious law firm in Chicago. As she is always striving for more, Mary wrote this book after discovering her college journals packed away in moving boxes and thought it would be helpful to share her experiences with those heading off to college. The journal excerpts contain lessons pertaining to life, love and personal growth, along with her commentary and hindsight. Adjusting to college life is difficult but may be just a little easier with this book by your side. Mary enjoys spending time with her family, attending concerts and staying active with her Peloton bike. Mary lives in Chicago with her husband, son and two rescue dogs.

To learn more,
- visit www.mary-reid.com
- follow Mary
  - mary_readingmymind on Instagram
  - maryreidauthor on Tik Tok
  - www.linkedin.com/in/maryreidauthor

The B Corp Movement

Dear reader,

Thank you for reading this book and joining the Publish Your Purpose community! You are joining a special group of people who aim to make the world a better place.

What's Publish Your Purpose About?

Our mission is to elevate the voices often excluded from traditional publishing. We intentionally seek out authors and storytellers with diverse backgrounds, life experiences, and unique perspectives to publish books that will make an impact in the world. Beyond our books, we are focused on tangible, action-based change. As a woman- and LGBTQ+-owned company, we are committed to reducing inequality, lowering levels of poverty, creating a healthier environment, building stronger communities, and creating high-quality jobs with dignity and purpose.

Certified

(B)

Corporation

As a Certified B Corporation, we use business as a force for good. We join a community of mission-driven companies building a more equitable, inclusive, and sustainable global economy. B Corporations must meet high standards of transparency, social and environmental performance, and accountability as determined by the nonprofit B Lab. The certification process is rigorous and ongoing (with a recertification requirement every three years).

How Do We Do This?

We intentionally partner with socially and economically disadvantaged businesses that meet our sustainability goals. We embrace and encourage our authors and employee's differences in race, age, color, disability, ethnicity, family or marital status, gender identity or expression, language, national origin, physical and mental ability, political affiliation, religion, sexual orientation, socio-economic status, veteran status, and other characteristics that make them unique.

Community is at the heart of everything we do—from our writing and publishing programs to contributing to social enterprise nonprofits like reSET (www.resetco. org) and our work in founding B Local Connecticut.

We are endlessly grateful to our authors, readers, and local community for being the driving force behind the equitable and sustainable world we are building together.

To connect with us online, or publish with us, visit us at www.publishyourpurpose.com.

Elevating Your Voice,

Jenn T Grace

Jenn T. Grace
Founder, Publish Your Purpose

www.ingramcontent.com/pod-product-compliance
Lightning Source LLC
Chambersburg PA
CBHW051208090426
42740CB00021B/3420